"Greg Wolfe has done something very remarkable for both the Christian community and the fractured, fractious culture we inhabit in the North Atlantic world. In his work as editor of the most energizing and imaginative periodical we have in the field of faith and the arts, he has continually reminded us all of why Christianity still draws the attention of the most imaginative spirits, orthodox and not-so-orthodox. These essays amply show how a theologically informed perspective can generate a serious, adult, joyful inhabiting of creation. They go well beyond journalistic polarities and never fail to give fresh light on our condition. A joy and an enrichment."

—ROWAN WILLIAMS, former archbishop of Canterbury

"Greg Wolfe's essays in *Image*—the latest batch having been collected here in *The Operation of Grace*—have a knack for getting the head and the heart in tune. Each of these essays is an invocation—an act of summoning, a preparation for transfigurations yet to come."

—ANNIE DILLARD, Pulitzer Prize-winning author of *Pilgrim at Tinker Creek*

"It's tempting to read Greg Wolfe as a voice speaking to us from an earlier age, when faith and culture were not antagonists, but two sides to the same coin. This would be a mistake: the humane, intelligent essays in *The Operation of Grace* exist to remind us that that time isn't past at all."

—CHRISTOPHER BEHA, author of *What Happened to Sophie Wilder*

"These 'occasional pieces' in fact add up to a marvelous whole—an erudite, provocative whole, at times winsome and at times bracing. They are abundant with wisdom about the pursuit of art, faith, and mystery (our pursuit of them, or, sometimes more properly, their pursuit of us). They are, in short, a gift."

—LAUREN F. WINNER, author of *Girl Meets God and Still*

"For over a quarter-century, Gregory Wolfe has been illuminating and fostering the sometimes overlooked but vital matrix upon which religion and art encounter one another, not just as belief and creative work but as a singular manifestation of 'real presence' in which God and beauty body forth as grace. This new collection of essays—wise, acute, and compelling—is a bold and necessary dispatch from an essential writer."

—ROBERT CLARK, author of *Mr. White's Confession and Dark Water*

THE OPERATION OF GRACE

5 December 2015

For Fr. David Leigh,

THE OPERATION OF
GRACE

with best wishes.

Further Essays
on Art, Faith, and Mystery

GREGORY WOLFE

CASCADE *Books* · Eugene, Oregon

THE OPERATION OF GRACE
Further Essays on Art, Faith, and Mystery

Cascade Books
An Imprint of Wipf and Stock Publishers
199 W. 8th Ave., Suite 3
Eugene, OR 97401

www.wipfandstock.com

ISBN 13: 978-1-62564-057-4

Cataloging-in-Publication data:

Wolfe, Gregory.

The operation of grace : further essays on art, faith, and mystery / Gregory Wolfe.

xiv + 208 p.; 23 cm.

ISBN 13: 978-1-62564-057-4

1. Religion and the arts. 2. Humanity. 3. Culture. 4. Criticism, interpretation. I. Title.

MLCS 2015/02436 (B)

Manufactured in the USA.

Contents

For Mary Kenagy Mitchell

Preface: A Metaphorical God

"My God, my God, thou art a direct God, may I not say a literal God, a God that wouldst be understood literally and according to the plain sense of all that thou sayest? but thou art also . . . a figurative, a metaphorical God too; a God in whose words there is such a height of figures, such voyages, such peregrinations to fetch remote and precious metaphors, such extensions, such spreadings, such curtains of allegories, such third heavens of hyperboles, so harmonious elocutions, so retired and so reserved expressions, so commanding persuasions, so persuading commandments, such sinews even in thy milk, and such things in thy words, as all profane authors seem of the seed of the serpent that creeps, thou art the Dove that flies."

—JOHN DONNE, *Devotions upon Emergent Occasions*

THE ESSAYS GATHERED IN this volume were originally published as editorial statements, each beginning an issue of the literary quarterly *Image*. They seek to explore the trinity of terms we've set forth in the journal's subtitle, "art, faith, mystery." Whether these words strike you as intriguing or pretentious may depend on your personal tastes, but anyone proposing them for consideration ought to have an explanation or two handy for the curious.

In the early days of *Image* the subtitle was the more prosaic and scholarly sounding "A Journal of the Arts and Religion." It was serviceable enough, but for a literary quarterly featuring original creative work rather than scholarship, it gave the wrong impression. Not to mention that it lacked something in the way of connotative richness. And since art works its magic through that sort of suggestiveness, we felt the need to make a change. Then we noticed some publications using individual words, staccato fashion, as subtitles to suggest a whole realm of interrelated interests, and we pondered what words might work for *Image*.

"Art" was a given, and once again it needed to come first. For all its power—and no doubt *because* of its power—art through the centuries has often been harnessed to powerful interests, religious as well as political. The cornerstone of *Image*'s vision has been the conviction that art can explore religious experience in ways that are neither didactic nor moralistic. To paraphrase Walker Percy, we believe that art is cognitive—that it is a way of knowing and embodying, in dramatic form, an encounter with reality. Art is not beholden to some other language or discipline for its capacity to discover and convey meaning.

We chose "faith" instead of "religion" because it felt like a more active and immersive word—more existential, less like a philosophical category. However dogged by doubt one's faith may be, it is ultimately a verb as much as a noun—an ongoing (if fraught and daunting) act rather than something static and settled. And to the extent that faith sounds like a verb, it reverberates, so to speak, with the word *art*, reminding us of the importance of art as making, an ongoing creative act.

As you might imagine, the third term proved the trickiest. After all, the first two words establish a trajectory, lines of convergence. What might the common endpoint be? It didn't take us long to set aside "spirituality," not only because it is a term so watered down and anodyne as to have become meaningless, but also because it denied art's cognitive power and threatened to strap it back into the harness again, reducing art to therapy.

We settled on "mystery," though we're aware that to some ears it might sound like little more than mystification. But in the past half-century Flannery O'Connor and a number of leading modern philosophers and theologians rescued the concept of mystery from near oblivion, demonstrating that it has deep roots in nearly all of the world's religious traditions.

What appealed to us was that mystery simultaneously conveys an adumbration of transcendence—Rudolph Otto's *mysterium tremendum*—and a form of knowing. The Greek *mysterion* derives from a word meaning "to shut" or "to close," but in most of the ancient religions one could undergo a series of rituals and practices that would, in time, nudge the door open just enough to allow in a little light.

Thus mystery lies in the borderland between the knowable and the unknowable. "For we know in part," as Saint Paul put it. Through the glass, darkly.

It would be easy (and lazy) to simply say that mystery is suprarational and leave it at that. But that does a disservice to reason, which is just another way of saying that we have an inbuilt desire for the world to make sense. Mystery thus lies at the intersection where reason, intuition, and imagination meet and only the both/and language of paradox seems capable of uniting everything that otherwise seems hopelessly either/or. We are body and soul, bound and free, fallen and godlike.

In *Real Presences* the critic George Steiner likened this place of mystery to Holy Saturday, another emblem of in-betweenness, after the crucifixion but before the resurrection:

> But ours is a long day's journey of the Saturday. Between suffering, aloneness, unutterable waste on the one hand and the dream of liberation, of rebirth on the other. In the face of the torture of a child, of the death of love which is Friday, even the greatest art and poetry are almost helpless. In the Utopia of the Sunday, the aesthetic will, presumably, no longer have logic or necessity. The apprehensions and figurations in the play of metaphysical imagining, in the poem and the music, which tell of pain and of hope, of the flesh which is said to taste of ash and of the spirit which is said to have the savor of fire, are always Sabbatarian. They have risen out of an immensity of waiting which is that of man. Without them, how could we be patient?

In some ways, *mystery* is perhaps the boldest term, the one most out of touch with our times. It is true that secular artists and writers regularly speak of navigating the uncertainties and ambiguities in the world. But in their embrace of post-Enlightenment thought, they tacitly accept various determinisms that attempt to explain reality with reference to biology, psychology, sociology, or any of the modernist replacements for ultimate reality. Most secular writers and artists simply live with the contradiction and avoid dealing with it. Though there occasionally arise writers like David Foster Wallace who are more open and anguished about these conflicts, a tendency toward evasion and complacency remains the norm.

At the same time it is no exaggeration to say that much of the contemporary hostility toward mystery comes from those who enthusiastically embrace religion. The relentless literalism and pragmatism of the fundamentalist stem from a fear of mystery, of the ambiguity of living on Holy Saturday. In the decades since *Image* was founded there have been salutary changes among believers who have awakened to the severe limitations of politics and polemics and embraced the need to make culture, not war. But there is still a long, long way to go.

In the preface to my first collection of *Image* essays, *Intruding upon the Timeless*, I focused largely on one aspect of the journal's mission: the ambition to prove that the encounter between art and faith was far from extinct, that it continued in our own time and all over the globe. That desire to find a place at the table in the larger cultural conversation was, indeed, central to the founding of the journal. The goal was not to engage secularism and fundamentalism in a new culture war, but to demonstrate that an ancient and still vital alternative tradition remains worthy of engagement.

More than a quarter century into the experiment, I think it's fair to say that we're only just beginning that conversation.

But it's also fair to say that those of us who started the journal sensed in a dim and inchoate way that we were after something larger than a place at the table. At some level we realized that placing art and faith in dialogue would produce powerful resonances.

It's turned out to be one hell of a tuning fork. Each of those resonances is really an analogy—a comparison that, while acknowledging differences, still finds illuminating resemblances. For example, what might the literary device known as ambiguity have to say about the life of faith? Is tragedy compatible with the ways that Western religions imagine the deity? How might reading Scripture influence the way we read novels, or paintings for that matter?

Art and faith use narrative, language, image, and symbol like probes sent out to take readings and return with reports of meaning. They share a need to initiate acts of making and discovery that, far from knowing in advance what they will encounter, must proceed in fear and trembling.

Analogy is a complex subject. In the *Summa Theologiae*, Thomas Aquinas considers whether poetic analogy can tell us anything true about God, given the utter disparity between human and divine minds:

> The science of poetry is about things which because of their deficiency of truth cannot be laid hold of by reason. Hence reason has to be drawn off to the side by means of certain similitudes. But then, theology is also about things which lie beyond reason. Thus the symbolic method is common to both, since neither is accommodated [to human reason].

The specific question that Aquinas grapples with is the way in which Scripture employs metaphors—which are, after all, analogies. He concludes that:

> the beam of divine revelation is not extinguished by the sense imagery that veils it; its truth does not flicker out; because the minds

of those to whom the revelation is given are not allowed to remain arrested by the images but are lifted up to their meaning.

I take these quotations from Denis Donoghue's dense but rewarding book *Metaphor*. There he considers the famous definition of metaphor by I. A. Richards as something divided into "tenor" and "vehicle." For example, in Shakespeare's phrase "all the world's a stage," *world* is the tenor and *stage* is the vehicle. The best metaphors, Donoghue suggests, set up a tension of likeness and unlikeness between tenor and vehicle: "Metaphor is the mutual relation of tenor and vehicle, a relation achieved by holding the two simultaneously in one's mind."

Donoghue notes that in the Christian tradition some thinkers seemed to believe that the vehicle takes over and extinguishes the tenor, as in those theologians who argued that the New Testament made the Old Testament obsolete and irrelevant. But he goes on to show that the deepest and widest tradition in the church rejected this form of reductionism, cherishing both terms equally. He cites Erich Auerbach, who points out in *Mimesis* that Tertullian spoke for the majority of theologians:

> He [Tertullian] was definitely hostile to spiritualism and refused to consider the Old Testament as mere allegory; according to him, it had real, literal meaning throughout, and even where there was figural prophecy, the figure had just as much historical reality as what it prophesied. The prophetic figure, he believed, is a concrete historical fact, and it is fulfilled by concrete historical facts.

For Auerbach, figurative language "establishes a connection between two events or persons, the first of which signifies not only itself but also the second, while the second encompasses or fulfills the first." In the poet Dante, Auerbach found the literary culmination of this way of thinking:

> It is precisely the figural interpretation of reality which, though in constant conflict with purely spiritualist and Neoplatonic tendencies, was the dominant view in the European Middle Ages: the idea that earthly life is thoroughly real, with the reality of the flesh into which the Logos entered, but that with all its reality it is only umbra and figura of the authentic, future, ultimate truth, the real reality that will unveil and preserve the figura.

It is in this spirit, if on a thoroughly pedestrian level, that I have attempted to pursue the analogies between art and faith in search of mystery.

This time around I've attempted to group the essays into thematic sections in hope of making the book more approachable. Of course the placement of many of these essays remains somewhat arbitrary. The piece I've chosen to begin the collection is one that goes back to ancient cave art, where the analogies begin.

Orcas Island, July 11, 2015
Feast of Saint Benedict

PROLOGUE:
RETURNING TO THE CAVE

The Cave and the Cathedral

IN 1994, THREE SPELUNKERS were looking for undiscovered caves in the Ardèche region of southeastern France. The region is named after the Ardèche River, which has cut through limestone for millennia and created hundreds of caves. On a summer weekend expedition they came across a place in a cliff wall where they sensed a draft of warm air near a pile of rubble. They dug around it but soon lost interest. Then in December they returned to the same place and felt a stronger draft. They began digging in earnest and entered a vast cave complex filled with dozens of cave bear skulls (a species that has been extinct for 12,000 years) and hundreds of prehistoric drawings on the walls—drawings of such breathtaking beauty they knew they had made a major discovery. Two of the spelunkers chose to name the cave after the third, Jean-Marie Chauvet, who had been exploring the region for three decades.

Like many people, I first learned about Chauvet Cave through the Werner Herzog documentary *Cave of Forgotten Dreams*. It's a typical Herzog film—personal and eccentric, marked by moments of insight and marred by a number of strange non sequiturs—but it may be the best footage of this cave the world is ever likely to see, given the French government's decision to refuse public access to it. When I saw the handheld camera lights illuminate the first image on the wall, I found myself transfixed.

Several things make Chauvet stand out among prehistoric cave sites. For one thing, the majority of the animals depicted are not those that would have been hunted for food, such as aurochs and mammoths. Rather, there are dozens of depictions of major predators like cave bears, woolly rhinoceros, cave lions, panthers, and cave hyenas.

But what really caused me to hold my breath was that this cave art was unmistakably art. These charcoal drawings are not mere stick figures; they employ shading and smudging that model three dimensions and perspective. One of the bison is rendered not in profile, but turned toward the viewer, looking out from under a thick matting of fur. A cave bear's bulk and musculature is suggested by the alternating use of thick and thin lines. An owl, traced by a finger in clay, has its head swiveled 180 degrees, looking at us over its folded wings. A rhinoceros is depicted in cubist fashion—with multiple legs and a series of echoed horns—capturing movement in a single image. One of the creatures in the "Panel of Horses" is open mouthed, as if neighing loudly. A pride of lions crouches low to the ground as they hunt unsuspecting bison. Several of the drawings deliberately use the shape of the wall to emphasize the contours of what they are portraying. The other distinctive: though there has been some debate, scientists now generally believe that Chauvet may be over 30,000 years old, nearly twice as old as the cave art at Lascaux and Altamira.

What makes all this so compelling to me is that it runs counter to the received wisdom. Since the Enlightenment we've been told by anthropologists that art by early humans was utilitarian in purpose: cave art, they argued, was part of a shamanic ritual in which pictures of animals enabled hunters to gain power over the animals' spirits and thus kill them more effectively.

The same goes for the religious dimension of Paleolithic humanity, which is seen as little more than the manipulation of the environment. When an anthropologist in *Cave of Forgotten Dreams* is asked what constitutes our humanness, all he can say is "the capacity for adaptation," a purely functional explanation.

The operative word in the received wisdom has always been *power*—power over those animal spirits, power over the environment. But this seems to me to project the ideology of modern scientism—Francis Bacon's conviction that science involves power over nature—on rich, complex, ancient phenomena. It's hard to imagine anything less scientific than projecting a prejudice onto the evidence. But when I gaze at the drawings on the walls of Chauvet—when I see male and female cave lions (predators unlikely to become the Paleolithic tribe's next meal) shown gently brushing up against one another—all I can see is love. Welling up within this love I see wonder, awe, praise, and celebration—art that generates life, rather than seeking to take it away.

It is as if the artists sense in these beasts beings who are similar to themselves and yet mysteriously different—strange and enchanting cousins in the order of creation. Emblems of beauty, strength, speed, passion. If, as the saying goes, love is the opposite of power, then the underlying motive behind art—the re-creation of the world—is something closer to Lewis Hyde's notion of art as gift, offering, sacrifice. When Jean-Marie Chauvet and his friends entered the cave for the first time they came upon a block of stone that had fallen from the roof, and on that stone was the skull of a cave bear pointing toward them. What they saw was an altar.

The heart of our humanness is not merely the capacity for adaptation but the ability to perceive and make meaning, to experience the world as an altar upon which the divine enters flesh. From the proverbial dawn of time we have felt the need to withdraw from the bright glare of sunlight and enter into a dark space where we can re-imagine the world, drawing it on cave walls and embedding it in stained glass, where it can be contemplated by torchlight and candlelight. To truly encounter what is to be found in Chauvet, even vicariously through film and photographs, is to suddenly realize that words like *art* and *religion* are clumsy, ham-fisted abstractions that violate something whole and ultimately inviolable. It also tends to make the word *primitive*, with all the connotations that have grown up around it over the centuries, seem almost laughable, if not obscene.

One of the researchers interviewed in *Cave of Forgotten Dreams* seems to understand this. In order to understand Chauvet, he says, you must go outside to other ancient cultures. He then relates the story of an ethnographer who accompanied an Australian Aborigine on an expedition to some very old rock paintings. The paintings had decayed because no one had continued the tradition of touching them up. This made the Aborigine sad, so he began to touch up the pictographs. The ethnographer asked him: "Why are you painting?"

The Aborigine answered: "I am not painting."

What's at stake here is nothing less than the nature of consciousness itself. Owen Barfield, one of the most incisive thinkers on this subject, once said: "Before the scientific revolution the world was more like a garment men wore about them than a stage on which they moved." The Aborigine's response is indicative of what Barfield calls "original participation," characteristic of early humanity—an unselfconscious sense of unity between observer and observed, man and nature.

In his book *Saving the Appearances* Barfield notes that Greek philosophy and the religion of Israel profoundly changed the dimensions of participation. Both of these cultures pulled back from mythic consciousness, one through reason and the other through monotheism. For example, while the golden calf could be said to represent original participation, the

Israelites felt they had to reject it. But this only changed the shape of participation: for them the discovery that God is not in the wind or the earthquake or the fire meant that he must be perceived as the mystery behind all of creation—that the mystery in some sense was more truly like each one of them, singular and personal.

Barfield holds that this new phase, far from eliminating participation, made it more inward. The synthesis of Greek reason and Hebrew monotheism in the Christian era (both stressing the need for human participation in a divine order through prayer and contemplation) continued through the Middle Ages. But with the scientific revolution, man separated himself from nature and embraced an abstract way of thinking. The modern West, Barfield says, exchanged meaning for literalism, turning the things of this world from signs into idols. Creation became a series of objects which operated like a machine. He illustrates this by imagining a clever child who is put inside an automobile. If he plays around with the instruments long enough he will be able to drive the car, but he will have only "dashboard knowledge," not true knowledge of the car.

This could be taken as nothing more than a narrative of decline, but Barfield believes that even as modern, self-conscious individuals we can still experience what he calls "final participation." Ironically, this is where those clumsy abstractions "art" and "religion" return, because for Barfield final participation comes through the creation of metaphor. He points to the Romantics, who sought to move beyond the mechanistic deism of the eighteenth century and reconnect to nature as an organic unity—only to fall into a sort of sentimental pantheism. Barfield's friends C. S. Lewis and J. R. R. Tolkien were engaged in a struggle to redeem Romanticism by grounding it in a more traditional theology.

Flannery O'Connor understood this at an even deeper level. Near the end of her novel *Wise Blood*, after the formerly nihilistic protagonist, Hazel Motes, has experienced traumatic humiliation and begun a series of penitential practices, there is a description of his landlady, Mrs. Flood. Increasingly disturbed by Hazel's acts of penance, she worries that he has become like "a monk in a monkery." This offends Mrs. Flood's enlightened view of the world. "She liked the clear light of day. She liked to see things." But Hazel, who once preached against the possibility of participation, now presents her with a mystery.

> She could not make up her mind what would be inside his head and what out. She thought of her own head as a switchbox where

6

she controlled from; but with him, she could only imagine the outside in, the whole black world in his head and his head bigger than the world, his head big enough to include the sky and planets and whatever was or had been or would be. How would he know if time was going backwards or forwards or if he was going with it? She imagined it was like you were walking in a tunnel and all you could see was a pinpoint of light. She had to imagine the pinpoint of light; she couldn't think of it at all without that. She saw it as some kind of star, like the star on Christmas cards. She saw him going backwards to Bethlehem and she had to laugh.

Few of us these days are immune from thinking of our heads as switch boxes from which we operate the machinery of our lives, whether we are aware of it or not. That's the world we inherit. But the world of objects, the world of mechanism, the dashboard knowledge that has us all speeding around in circles, is hollow at the core, a desecrated altar, an abomination of desolation.

The good news is that a life of participation, however fitfully experienced, is still possible for us, albeit through discipline and effort. We can go back into the darkness of the cave and offer up our broken re-creations of the world on an altar and know that the broken, sacrificed god will meet us there.

We can walk backward to Bethlehem.

ART SPEAKS TO FAITH

The Wound of Beauty

STRANGE AS IT MAY seem, beauty still needs to be defended. In the history of the West, beauty has played the role of Cinderella to her sisters, goodness and truth. I don't mean to say that beauty in art or nature hasn't been appreciated throughout history—though there have been times when beauty has been the subject of frontal assaults—but simply that when we start getting official, when we get theological or philosophical, beauty becomes a hot potato.

The ambivalence about beauty at the heart of Western culture begins at the beginning. In Jerusalem, proscriptions against idols and graven images coexist with paeans to the craftsmanship of God and Bezalel, the artificer (described in Exodus) of the desert tabernacle. In Athens, Plato celebrates the divine madness that the poet experiences when the muse descends, but he also kicks the poets out of his ideal republic as unreliable, disruptive sorts.

In theory, goodness, truth, and beauty—traditionally known as the "transcendentals," because they are the three qualities that God has in infinite abundance—are equal in dignity and worth. Indeed, in Christian thought there has always been a sense that the transcendentals exist in something of a trinitarian relationship to one another. But in practice it rarely seems to work out that way.

The funny thing is that secular and religious attacks on beauty are nearly identical. Beauty is seen as an anesthetizing force that distracts us from the moral imperatives of justice and the quest for truth. There isn't much difference between a stern proponent of Iconoclasm in the eighth century and a modern Marxist attacking beauty as nothing but an opiate to lull us into acquiescence to the powers that be. Both critics abhor what Wendy Steiner has called "the scandal of pleasure."

The time has come to bring beauty back, to give it the glass slipper and invite it to the prom.

The thinker who has helped me most along these lines is the twenti-eth-century theologian Hans Urs von Balthasar. His argument—and it is a rather unsettling one—is that of the three transcendentals, beauty is the one that is least troubled by our fallen condition. In a world plagued by sin and error, he says, truth and goodness are always hotly contested. How do you live righteously? What is the truth? As we debate these matters, we have axes to grind.

But beauty, von Balthasar says, is disinterested. It has no agenda. Beauty can sail under the radar of our anxious contention over what is true and what is good, carrying along its beam a ray of the beatific vision. Beauty can pierce the heart, wounding us with the transcendent glory of God.

Von Balthasar's magnum opus, *The Glory of the Lord,* is structured in three parts, corresponding to the three transcendentals. He stresses the importance of the order in which he discusses them:

> Beauty is the word which shall be our first. Beauty is the last thing which the thinking intellect dares to approach since only it dances as an uncontained splendor around the double constellation of the true and the good and their inseparable relation to one another. Beauty is the disinterested one, without which the ancient world refused to understand itself, a word which both imperceptibly and unmistakably has bid farewell to our new world, a world of inter-ests, leaving it to its own avarice and sadness. No longer loved or fostered by religion, beauty is lifted from its face as a mask, and its absence exposes features on that face which threaten to become incomprehensible to man. We no longer dare to believe in beauty, and we make of it a mere appearance in order the more easily to dispose of it. Our situation today shows that beauty demands for itself at least as much courage and decision as do truth and good-ness, and she will not allow herself to be separated and banned from her two sisters without taking them along with herself in an act of mysterious vengeance. We can be sure that whoever sneers at her name, as if she were the ornament of a bourgeois past, whether he admits it or not, can no longer pray and soon will no longer be able to love.

A quotation as dense with meaning as that is a hard act to follow. But one of the more intriguing suggestions made by von Balthasar concerns that "act of mysterious vengeance." When you remove beauty from the human equation, it is going to come back in some other form, even as anti-beauty. A good deal of modern art can be understood in this light. In modernity, beauty has been seen as an appearance—ornamentation, sugar coating. Secularists and believers alike have either rejected beauty altogether or argued that beauty should make the pills of truth and goodness go down easier. Beauty must serve some other end; it is not an end in itself.

But the transcendentals were always understood as infinitely valuable, as ends in themselves. When it comes to beauty, however, we are afraid to assert that much. We feel the need to harness it, because beauty is unpredictable, wild.

Here's how I have tried to comprehend these deep matters. If you think about these three transcendentals in relationship to our human capacities, what are the faculties that correspond to these three transcendentals? Goodness, I would say, has to do with faith, the desire for holiness. Truth is pursued by reason.

We are all familiar with that pairing: faith and reason. That's standard-issue language in the Western tradition. But what about the third element? What faculty does beauty correspond to? I would suggest that it is the imagination. The imagination is the faculty honed to apprehend beauty and unfold its meaning.

How often do we say the Judeo-Christian tradition is a tradition of faith, reason, and imagination? This is what I mean by saying that we treat beauty as the Cinderella. "Go make pretty pictures," we say to beauty, "but don't start acting like you are a pathway to knowing the universe."

Yet this is precisely what the definition of a transcendental means. That's easy to see when it comes to truth. But the same applies to goodness: when we act justly, we come to know more about reality. And so it is with beauty. Beauty allows us to penetrate reality through the imagination, through the capacity of the imagination to perceive the world intuitively.

Seeing the Form—that is the title of the first volume of von Balthasar's trilogy. Aesthetics comes from the Greek word for perception, *aisthesis*. Saint Thomas Aquinas defined beauty as "id quod visum placet"—that which being seen, pleases. A work of art has a flash of radiance about it that we find pleasurable, but the pleasure comes from our recognition of *meaning*, a pattern within our normally chaotic experience.

The intuitive perception of meaning that art provides helps us to see that imagination is akin to reason: both seek truth through the apprehension of order and pattern. Art employs beautiful forms to generate objects that penetrate reality.

Beauty tends to elicit in us a type of shock. We draw a breath in. Why? If beauty tells us about the eternal verities, whence the surprise? Ezra Pound once said that the artist's task is to "make it new." The "it" is the truth of the world. A work of art doesn't invent truth, but it does make it accessible to us in ways that are not normally available because words and images have been tarnished by overuse or neglect. Art fails when it merely tells us what we already know in the ways that we already know it.

That is why art is so deeply related to the prophetic dimension and the place where it connects to truth. That prophetic shock, that challenge to complacency, that revelatory reconfiguration of the way things are, gives us a truer picture of the way that the world is.

Truth without beauty is fleshless abstraction, a set of propositions. Only beauty can incarnate truth in concrete, believable, human flesh.

Beauty also has the capacity to help us to value the good, especially the goodness of the most ordinary things. The greatest epics, the most terrible tragedies, all have one goal: to bring us back to the ordinary and help us to love and to cherish it. Odysseus encounters Circe, Cyclops, the sirens, Scylla, and Charybdis, but his real destination is home and the marital bed that makes it his place in the world.

That is the magic of art. It may spread a huge canvas, it may be bold and baroque, but its essence is to remind us of the everyday and to transmute it into a sacrament.

Beauty tutors our compassion, making us more prone to love and to see the attraction of goodness. Art takes us out of our self-referentiality and invites us to see through the eyes of the other, whether that other is the artist herself or a character in a story. Because beauty endows goodness with mercy, it enables us to see how difficult it is to achieve goodness, how often one good exists in tension with another. Our pursuit of the good is inherently dramatic, and drama is based on conflict.

Thus goodness without beauty is moralism, holier than thou.

At the same time, it is only fair to say that beauty without truth is a lie. Beauty without truth becomes the mask that von Balthasar speaks of, a mask that has no relationship to the face behind it.

Beauty without goodness is frigid and lifeless. It can be pure virtuosity—form without meaning—but then it fails to touch the heart. We admire the acrobatics but fail to see the point.

Perhaps it goes without saying, but any serious discussion of beauty needs to treat it as something more than prettiness. The Greeks, as I have suggested, were deeply divided about beauty. They loved harmony, proportion, symmetry, the ideal form. But they also knew darkness, as their tragedies attest.

To my mind, a deeper understanding of beauty came into being with Christianity. The cross, the instrument of torture and shame, was taken up into a higher vision of beauty. Brokenness and woundedness—the shattering of the ideal—can become the means whereby beauty is revealed. Here is a beauty that is anything but sentimental. It is akin to what Yeats meant by his phrase "a terrible beauty." Lest we forget, the glorified body of the risen Christ still bears the marks of his wounds.

Beauty itself wounds us, pierces our hearts, opens us up. Let us, then, free it to dance in "uncontained splendor around the double constellation of the true and the good."

The Tragic Sense of Life

When I first arrived at Oxford University in the early 1980s to pursue graduate work, I was all swagger on the outside, but that was to conceal the soft center of terror within. I had gone from being a big man on a small midwestern campus situated between two cornfields to a nobody at an ancient European university whose "New College" had been founded in the fifteenth century. For one thing, there were the social bewilderments attendant upon entering a society where class was a more important and more complex phenomenon than I had ever known it could be. But in the end my greatest fears were centered on academic performance. I remember in particular being crushed by my tutor's response to my essay on *King Lear*. My argument had been something to the effect that the tragedy of Lear's humiliation and Cordelia's death was mitigated by the spiritual insights these two characters had gained. In particular, I pointed out the Christian implications of Lear's famous words to Cordelia:

> Come, let's away to prison:
> We two alone will sing like birds i' the cage:
> When thou dost ask me blessing, I'll kneel down,
> And ask of thee forgiveness: so we'll live,
> And pray, and sing, and tell old tales, and laugh
> At gilded butterflies, and hear poor rogues
> Talk of court news; and we'll talk with them too,
> Who loses and who wins; who's in, who's out;
> And take upon's the mystery of things,
> As if we were God's spies. . . .

My tutor, who combined a gentle and kindly soul with a bear-trap of a mind, suggested that perhaps I was sentimentalizing what was in fact a shatteringly bleak ending—that I was missing the savage, tragic irony of the play. After all, he said, Cordelia is executed right after this speech and Lear himself dies from the shock. Within moments he is screaming "Howl, howl, howl" and is then himself dead, dead, dead. The play, my tutor reminded me, was deliberately set by Shakespeare in pagan times, so the characters have no access to Christian consolation, no heaven to right earthly wrongs and make everything better.

I don't recall whether I blushed, but I was immediately overcome by both shame and gratitude. I not only sensed the merit of his challenge but I also felt liberated. My youthful, earnest religiosity had imposed itself on the text, papering over an abyss of waste and horror with innocuous pieties.

Naturally, this got me thinking, not only about the way that religion can become a set of blinders, but about my own experience, which had involved its share of personal tragedy. It also set me on a search for a faith that can encompass tragedy without reducing it to a meaningless episode, something left behind and forgotten in the larger story of redemption.

Over the intervening years I've become convinced that we all refuse tragedy at our peril, whether we are believers or not. The strange truth is that tragedy is largely absent from the pews and bookstores of the post-modern West. We study it in old books and plays, and we use it casually to refer to plane crashes and early deaths from cancer, but the full-blooded thing itself is gone.

The absence of the tragic sense of life is killing us.

In the culture I know best, that of the United States, tragedy is something that our founders believed they were leaving behind forever. They saw our shores as the new Eden. As it says on the back of the dollar bill, ours was to be a *novus ordo seclorum*, a "new order of the ages," free from the dark and bloody entanglements of Europe. Farewell, *ancien regime*. At the opposite end of the scale from the finality of tragedy is the myth of reinvention.

To refuse tragedy is to refuse to live in history, for history is the story of conflicts and injustices that cannot be merely undone. Perhaps that is why America believes it can help to reinvent other nations: history is not an obstacle.

As I listened to the radio a scant six hours after the space shuttle Challenger had broken up over the skies of Texas, a NASA engineer came to the microphone and said: "We can fix this." After 9/11 we pondered military strategies. Today we not only deny tragedy; we hardly pause to mourn. Not when the can-do spirit is on the line.

As tempting as it may be to lay the blame for tragedy's demise at the door of an impoverished religious sensibility, I have to say that secular modernity is also indifferent to the tragic sense. Where are the great tragic masterpieces of modernity? Where are the symposia in the *New York Review of Books* on the death of tragedy?

My intuition (and perhaps the beginning of a mature response to my tutor) is that tragedy is only possible when the deepest metaphysical questions are still available to us. If meaning is socially constructed, there can be no cosmological baseline against which to register a tragic circumstance. One man's tragedy is another man's farce. From Aeschylus, Sophocles, and Euripides to Dante, Milton, Shakespeare, and Racine, tragedy only makes sense when we can ask the questions that theodicy asks: why does suffering often seem to be out of proportion to guilt; where are the gods, or God, in what seems to be an unjust cosmos; how is it, to use Lear's words, that we are "more sinned against than sinning"?

I recently asked the literary critic Alan Jacobs where he finds tragedy in contemporary literature. His response is that the form has left the West and migrated to the global South. In particular, he singled out the Nigerian writers Wole Soyinka, Chinua Achebe, and Ben Okri.

The one American writer whose work I believe rises to tragic stature is Cormac McCarthy, at least in his Border Trilogy, and this is in part because these novels are about the confrontation between American characters and the global South as found in Mexican culture. The protagonists are true American heroes—you might call them the last cowboys, anachronisms surviving into the nuclear age. They are everything cowboys should be: self-reliant, laconic, courageous, attuned to nature, willing to fight for what is just. And when they cross the border into Mexico they become entangled in tragic circumstances from which they cannot extricate themselves.

Take John Grady's odyssey in the first book, *All the Pretty Horses*. Displaced from his grandfather's ranch, he goes to Mexico in search of opportunity—especially if that means working with horses. No sooner does John Grady cross the border than he is confronted by his comic double, a bony youngster named Jimmy Blevins who has run away from an abusive home. When the frightened child-man Jimmy loses his horse during a lightning storm, he is determined to get it back, though the Mexicans who find it are unwilling to give it up. The cost of his ill-fated quest will have terrible consequences not only for himself but also for Grady.

But if John Grady seems to tower above Jimmy Blevins in depth of soul, he pursues a similar quest to fix things, to restore what was lost, even if the cost involves the possibility of violence. McCarthy allows the reader to see Mexico as a place of lawlessness and treachery, and yet there are innumerable small hints that it possesses a generosity and wisdom America lacks. The Americans, individualists who think in terms of property and its restoration, fail to register the hospitality and communalism of the Mexicans. John Grady believes that he loses his paramour, the daughter of the *padron* on the ranch where he works, thanks to Jimmy Blevins. But in reality he could never have had her: too much history, class, and culture separate them. He cannot fathom the idea that powerful forces beyond his control can only be endured and not fixed.

A broken man at the end of the novel, John Grady wakes one morning, shivering and alone. He sees a group of Mexican peasants. One asks him where his serape is. When John Grady answers that he has none, "The man loosed the blanket from his own shoulders and swung it in a slow veronica and handed it to him." The word "veronica" here comes from bullfighting, where the toreador swirls the cape around. But of course Veronica ("true icon") is the traditional name for the woman in the Gospel whose cloth bears the imprint of the suffering Christ on the road to Golgotha. John Grady's tragedy is that he cannot grasp the tragic sense of life. This man of action cannot see the heroism of the wizened old Mexican ladies kneeling beneath garish statues of the bloody crucified Christ, women who celebrate the Virgin Mary because of her active embrace of suffering. Like Oedipus's, John Grady's virtues blind him to his own limitations before the brute order of necessity.

It is precisely here that a true theology of tragedy can begin to take shape. The notion that Christianity is somehow alien to tragedy—that it is simply and straightforwardly "comic" because the resurrection makes for a happy ending—could not be more radically wrong. In his essay "Tragedy and Christian Faith," Hans Urs von Balthasar singles out three essential elements of tragedy: that the good things of the world cannot sustain themselves and are lost; that this places us in a position of contradiction or alienation; and that this condition is bound up with an "opaque guilt," in which individual moral responsibility cannot account for all suffering, leaving us subject to a mysterious "inherited curse."

According to von Balthasar, Christ does not banish tragedy but carries it into the heart of God. Christ "fulfills the contradiction of existence . . .

not by dissolving the contradiction but by bearing that affirmation of the human condition as it is through still deeper darknesses *in finem,* 'to the end,' as love."

> To go to the end means . . . not only entering total defeat, the total bankruptcy of all earthly power and every project of salvation, but to go to the end of the night of sin, in that descent into hell where the one who dies and the one who is dead come into an atemporal state of being lost, in which no more hope of an end is possible, nor even the possibility of looking back to a beginning. And this as the conclusion of a tragedy of earthly life that itself already stood under the law of contradiction: since God's omnipotence wished and was able to make itself known ontologically in the Incarnation as powerlessness and unutterable limitation.

This may sound grandly theological, but I would argue that it has the most concrete and far-reaching consequences for the way we experience the world. If faith is to remain true to experience and not become a sentimentalized blindness, it must be permeated by the tragic sense of life. Unless we can believe that God has willingly submitted himself to the harsh necessities of the created order, we will be helpless when those necessities lay us low. We can only lean in to these forces, and know that such a posture is not passivity but action of the profoundest sort. Passion is not passive.

My tutor was right to challenge my reading of *King Lear,* but is it possible to embrace the fullness of this tragedy and yet see in its darkness an echo of the divine self-emptying? I think so.

For von Balthasar the resurrection is not "in any way a fifth act with a happy ending" but a mysterious affirmation of a love that can bear tragedy to the end. That is why, in the forty days that followed it, Christ was not magically made whole but bore the marks of his passion, and would not rest until we placed our hands—and our hearts—inside them.

Singularly Ambiguous

SAMUEL JOHNSON, THE GREAT eighteenth-century critic, moralist, and wit, once said of the American revolutionaries: "How is it that we hear the loudest yelps for liberty among the drivers of [slaves]?" I don't know what Johnson's friend, Edmund Burke—a proponent of American independence—said in response, but I rather hope it was: "Touché."

While I can't match Johnson's epigrammatic waggery, I often find myself with similar sentiments these days about those who seek to defend "the West" from its perceived enemies. Whether implicitly or explicitly, these champions of Western civilization believe that in a time of war, terrorism, and uncertainty the only adequate response is that of singular, unswerving affirmation. To be of two minds about the moral condition of Western culture or the political decisions of those who act in its name is perceived as weakness, or a species of self-hatred.

In fairness, there are plenty of intellectuals out there who seem to regard the tradition rooted in Jerusalem and Athens as the equivalent of original sin, the root of all evil. There is no shortage of energy to spin the ideological merry-go-round.

What's wrong with this picture? The classical and Judeo-Christian visions, as I understand them, are undergirded by two inseparable insights: through reason or revelation universal moral truths can be discerned, but their application in human affairs is a complex process, fraught with dangers and temptations. In other words, the singularity of truth is always shadowed by the ambiguity of the fallen creatures who strive to incarnate it. And so the cardinal sin in each of these cultures was the same, whether it was called hubris or pride: an overconfident singularity. In the real world the paradox is that truths can come into conflict. Because we are not gods but limited beings, the sorting out of these conflicts is an unending task, one that can end in tragedy or modest, provisional victory.

Two of the central poets of the West, Virgil and Shakespeare, explored this paradox in epic stories about political foundings. *The Aeneid* is concerned with the founding of Rome. Aeneas is a man with an inexorable sense of duty that drives him forward to a heroic undertaking. When he encounters Dido, queen of Carthage, on his journey, their love affair threatens to derail his mission, and so he leaves her. Distraught, she gives in to chaotic emotion, *furor,* and ends her life.

Now it is possible to read this section of *The Aeneid* as the rejection of a private good in favor of a larger public good, and as the triumph of Apollonian reason over Dionysian emotion. But it requires a great deal of insensitivity to miss its tragic dimension, and the danger of political imperatives running roughshod over the human goods of the private sphere. Aeneas does not, in fact, escape unscathed. In a brilliant ironic twist at the end of this unfinished epic, Aeneas defeats his final antagonist, Turnus, in single combat on the battlefield. Instead of practicing magnanimity toward the vanquished, which Aeneas is told will be the prime Roman virtue, when he sees that Turnus is wearing the buckler of a fallen Roman, he savagely kills Turnus in a fit of *furor.* The very act that makes way for the founding of Rome is a contradiction of all that Rome is to stand for.

Shakespeare's *Henriad* traces the establishment of a British dynasty. The decadent Richard III is succeeded by the scheming Machiavellian Bolingbroke, a ruthless modern man who seizes power but remains haunted by the thought that the ancient cosmology is correct, and that he is guilty of a horrific impiety. Meanwhile, his son Prince Hal is off roistering about the kingdom with old Jack Falstaff, embracing the life of the common man. But after he defeats Hotspur in battle and becomes king, Hal rejects Falstaff, who dies pathetically and offstage.

There has been endless debate over Shakespeare's tetralogy, of course, but few could make much of a case for the final play, *Henry V,* as anything other than a letdown, if not an outright failure. Both as a play and film, it has been used to bolster patriotism, as Olivier's version did during World War II. But the Henry depicted in this play is anything but the singular savior of England: alternately chummy and brutal, he is an awkward lover and an implacable conqueror. The expansive joie de vivre of Prince Hal is replaced by a figure who claims ancient religious sanction but acts like his Machiavellian dad. The monolithic nature of political power leaves little space for the messiness of the private realm.

Virgil and Shakespeare show us that ambiguity, properly understood, preserves truth from turning into falsehood. What has made the West strong is its admission of weakness. Ambiguity and self-questioning have become the engines of reform.

This is why I so love the Renaissance humanist Thomas More, a true son of the West. Though often held up as a saint of singularity, he was, in fact, far more devoted to what his biographer Peter Ackroyd has called "doubleness." Robert Bolt in *A Man for All Seasons* captures this quality of More's, particularly in the scene where he tells his hot-headed future son-in-law, William Roper, that he would give the devil—and by extension any heretic or malefactor—the benefit of law. To Roper's protest that this is to put man's law above God's, More replies, "[L]et me draw your attention to a fact—I'm not God. The currents and eddies of right and wrong, which you find such plain sailing, I can't navigate. I'm no voyager. But in the thickets of the law, oh, there I'm a forester."

More eventually stepped out of the woods and placed his neck on the block. But his greatest gift to us may have been his skills as a forester.

Strange Pilgrims

IN HIS MASTERFUL BOOK *The Life You Save May Be Your Own*, Paul Elie has crafted a braided narrative about the lives and works of four twentieth-century American Catholic writers, all now canonical figures: Dorothy Day, Thomas Merton, Flannery O'Connor, and Walker Percy. The first sentence begins casually but ends with a kick: "In the photographs, they don't look like people who might make you want to change your life."

For those who know anything about this quartet, this statement is puzzling. In their youth, all four had read—and felt liberated by—the French neo-Thomist Jacques Maritain's *Art and Scholasticism*. In that short book—more a primer than an extended study—Maritain argued convincingly, and from a deeply Christian point of view, against the notion that art should be created for the purpose of moral edification. Following Saint Thomas, Maritain said that the end of art is the good of the made thing, the perfection of the form. In their unique ways, Day, Percy, Merton, and O'Connor followed suit, writing edgy, disturbing works that offended the pious within their own religious communion.

O'Connor gave us proud, grotesque characters (rather like herself) who seek to control the world around them, only to meet violent crises that offer them a redemptive choice. Percy's lonely melancholics seek to anesthetize themselves but are forced to set off on an existential search, dodging grace for a time but ultimately sidling up to it. Merton gives us himself, the zealous convert and reinventor of monasticism, slowly discovering that he is mouthing pieties; in order to restore life to his own tradition, he cross-fertilizes it with Eastern spirituality and political engagement. Day, too, tells her own story, that of a Bohemian intellectual whose ideas about helping the poor gain traction only when secular humanitarianism is replaced by divine charity.

Elie has grasped a paradoxical truth about the "School of the Holy Ghost," as one wag dubbed the group. They have caused many readers to want to change their lives: to convert to Christianity and/or Catholicism; to become politically active; to study and practice ancient forms of Eastern and Western spirituality.

Elie makes no attempt to solve the paradox, but his richly detailed narrative sheds a great deal of light on the ways these writers balanced art and morality, orthodoxy and openness, the skeptical subjectivism of modern man with the objective claims of church and dogma. Elie contends that what all four had in common was a vision of human life as pilgrimage. He writes: "A pilgrimage is a journey undertaken in the light of a story. A great event has happened; the pilgrim hears the reports and goes in search of the evidence, aspiring to be an eyewitness. The pilgrim seeks not only to confirm the experience of others firsthand but to be changed by the experience."

Percy, with his concern for the way language can become cheapened and emptied of meaning through overuse and trivialization, preferred the word *wayfarer* to *pilgrim*. His own understanding was informed by Søren Kierkegaard's distinction between the genius and the apostle. The modern Romantic figure of the genius gave us a heroic figure who was capable of sudden epiphanies, personal revelations. But the apostle is someone who has "heard the news of something that has happened, and he has the authority to tell somebody who hasn't heard the news what the news is."

The writers covered in Elie's book defined themselves to a great extent as apostles to a secularized culture that had either lost or rejected the news. What made them so effective was that their art dramatized a search—a pilgrimage—in which distant rumors are verified through hard-won personal experience. This also set them apart from so many overtly religious folk who seem to feel that no pilgrimage is necessary, since they have already attained the promised land. The School of the Holy Ghost was orthodox but never tame or complacent.

In the fifteen years since *Image* was founded, the more monolithic, militant secularism that dominated the last century has given way to greater openness to religious experience as a path toward truth. A host of gifted writers and artists have traced journeys similar to those undertaken by Elie's quartet.

But here's another paradox: as religion and spirituality have become more popular, so have the number of those who seem to prefer the model of genius to that of apostle. Under the influence of postmodernism and the therapeutic mentality, these artists seem less interested in listening for news than in making it. To paraphrase Luigi Giussani, the founder of the lay Catholic movement known as Communion and Liberation, the new religious geniuses confuse the religious sense that is planted so deeply in our hearts with faith itself. People like this are fond of saying that the search is more important than any possible goal.

There is a kernel of truth here, but there is also a critical difference. The pilgrim has heard a specific piece of news; she lives her life guided by the memory of an event. But her path also leads her toward a specific end. The pilgrim may spend her life on the road, striving toward a goal that is never fully reached in this life, but she sees it ahead of her. And while the pilgrim's personal experience is central, a pilgrimage is never undertaken in solitude. Pilgrims travel in groups; their shared memory and end form a bond of friendship that tests and unfolds the meaning of the journey. One false alternative to pilgrimage is the arrogant belief that one has arrived. But the other is wandering alone.

Secular Scriptures

ANY NEW BOOK ABOUT the relationship between the Bible and literature enters a crowded field, one strewn with masterworks by the likes of Robert Alter, Frank Kermode, Northrop Frye, and Gabriel Josipovici. So the bar is set high. Nicholas Boyle's *Sacred and Secular Scriptures: A Catholic Approach to Literature* clears that bar with room to spare. While the subtitle might put some readers on guard, Boyle proves a hospitable and respectful writer; at points the Catholic tradition takes center stage, but much of the book speaks with equal power and resonance to Jewish and Protestant traditions.

There is no disguising the intellectual rigor of *Sacred and Secular Scriptures,* which contains a survey of modern biblical interpretation and close readings of several literary classics. Boyle is aware that some will be daunted by those sections of the book, so he makes the generous suggestion that readers pick and choose what to read. Impractical as that suggestion may be, I for one endorse it. The brief central section, "Sacred and Secular," could stand alone as a major contribution to the fields of theology, literary criticism, and aesthetics.

Drawing on the thought of Paul Ricoeur and Emmanuel Levinas, Boyle explores the ways in which both the Bible and secular literature might be understood as forms of revelation. Following Ricoeur, he defines revelation as "the manifestation to us of something that utilitarian reason could not possibly predict or infer or construct." In saying this, Boyle neither seeks to collapse the Bible into poetry or to undermine the historicity of any part of the Scriptures. What he does assert is that the two forms of writing involve poetic language that is nonpurposive and noninstrumental, words that:

> in different ways assert our freedom from the tyranny of function-
> al, goal-directed thought and language: secular literature by using
> words to give pleasure and so enabling us to enjoy what is; sacred
> literature by using words to utter obligation, and so to give us our

identity, not as beings who perform a function, but as creatures who know what ought to be.

Boyle is clear about what distinguishes the two forms of writing. The Bible reveals the fundamental moral obligation of the Law, the command that we love and care for the other. Secular literature, using the playful, entertaining forms of art, attempts to tell the truth about who we are and how we live. It cannot speak with the authority of divine revelation because it can be traced directly to individual authors, who are subject to historical and cultural contingencies in a manner that the Bible is not. Boyle relates the difference between sacred and secular literature to Kant's distinction between the beautiful and the moral: "the beautiful may be a symbol of morality, but the relation of symbolization implies difference and noncommensurability too."

Alike and yet incommensurable. Where, then, is the overlap between these forms of revelation? If there is "no literary simulacrum of the Law," as Boyle states, what relationship does secular literature have to divine truth?

To answer these questions, Boyle examines the nature of literary representation. The pleasure we take in literary mimesis, in the imitation of the world around us, lies in the public dimension of art. As Aristotle noted, the value of tragedy is the way it brings its viewers into a shared experience of grief and loss. In short, life matters. As Boyle puts it, "we are in it together."

In this sense, literature becomes "the secular analogue of the Redemption." Whether it is in the characters depicted in fiction and drama, or the persona of the speaker in poetry and creative nonfiction, literature tells the truth about both our noble origin and our fallenness. It represents a world worth loving and in need of forgiveness. Only in this way can literature be moral without being didactic.

Secular literature provides a commentary on the Bible. But here Boyle points out an interesting twist. It is in the nature of literary representation, he says, to strive for the appearance of the same authorlessness that characterizes sacred Scripture. "'These words are not being spun out of a mind, they tell truth' is the fiction, the lie, Plato would say, with which all fictions begin."

The tension at the heart of literature is between that striving for authority and an awareness of the limitations of the individual writer. In the third part of his book, Boyle traces this tension in Pascal's *Pensées*, Goethe's *Faust*, Melville's *Moby-Dick*, and Austen's *Mansfield Park*. Each of these works is modern, created at a time when the process of secularization in the West had begun. And so they serve as test cases for the existence of the secular as commentary on the sacred.

What Boyle finds in these works is the struggle against the limitations of secularity, one he detects in their difficult and enigmatic endings. But instead of seeing such conflicts as deconstructing the possibility of meaning, as a postmodern critic might, Boyle sees them in a more positive light:

> Read as showing Christ in the moment in which they mark themselves off from God, secular scriptures become the limit case of sacred scripture, the word of God no longer as an address to us—as God's reply to our prayer—but as the inarticulate groanings of the spirit within us—as our prayer itself.

A summary this abbreviated inevitably does an injustice to the original. Its virtue, I hope, is that it will send you to the source.

Shouts and Whispers

HAVING BEEN A PARTICIPANT in any number of roundtables and panels on the state of religion in America, and in particular the relationship between faith and culture, I've grown accustomed to hearing my conservative colleagues argue that contemporary writers of faith are flabby compared to the more muscular writers of the early- and mid-twentieth century.

The argument goes like this: writers like C. S. Lewis, W. H. Auden, Evelyn Waugh, and Flannery O'Connor created works that offered Christianity as an alternative to modern secularism. Many of them were public converts to the faith, and wrote works in which conversion is the central experience. By contrast, say these critics, writers who have religious concerns these days are more private, more inclined to doubt and ambiguity, more alienated from church authority—in short, ninety-eight-pound weaklings who get sand kicked in their faces.

It's an especially compelling argument for me because that generation of writers became my teachers and the shapers of my vocation. What I responded to in their writing was the way they discovered literary forms that avoided didacticism and suggested that the old Judeo-Christian tradition could hold its own against Marxism and Freudianism as a "master narrative." Without being triumphalistic this generation of writers used paradox and irony to sketch out a God-shaped silhouette. A reader might complain to Waugh that the Catholicism depicted in *Brideshead Revisited* seemed more like the "kiss of death" than a vibrant faith, but for Waugh that kiss was part of a larger vision: the strictures of the Church might seem to bring the characters only grief and loss, yet in the slow workings of grace that suffering would lead to something resembling happiness.

My hunch is that Waugh and his generation owed a large debt to High Modernism, which not only used irony and fragmentation but also epic myths and religious narratives to explore the loss and potential recovery of order.

By contrast, contemporary writers who engage religious faith fall more under the (admittedly problematic) heading of postmodernism: they're less sure they can, or should, create those big silhouettes. They're more interested in the scrimshaw of private life. Take, for example, Oscar Hijuelos in *Mr. Ives' Christmas* and Alice McDermott in *Charming Billy*—writers who offer us saints—not in the tragic/heroic mode of Graham Greene's whiskey priest, but in people whose holiness is furtive, buried deep within the quirks of their personalities.

So the argument that the modern/postmodern divide is about strength versus weakness has a certain plausibility. But the more I have struggled with this issue, the more I find myself returning to the metaphor at the heart of an essay published *Image* many years ago. The essay, by the novelist Doris Betts, is entitled "How to Whisper" and begins with a brief consideration of Flannery O'Connor's essay, "The Fiction Writer and His Country." There O'Connor makes her famous modernist aesthetic profession: "To the hard of hearing you shout, and for the almost-blind you have to draw large and startling figures."

While Betts loves O'Connor, she claims that her own artistic method involves whispers rather than shouts. "There's a range of times," Betts writes, "when Jesus inveighed strongly against a 'generation of vipers' and other times when he might stoop and silently scratch words in the ground." She continues:

> Like the descendants of Job's second cousins once removed, [my characters] struggle through a long weekday process that includes losses and boils until in the end God does not so much answer their questions as silence them, simply by being there, so that my characters end by saying—or maybe whispering—"Mine eye seeth Thee." Some of them might add: "That *is* You, isn't it?"

In the face of wisdom like this, those critics who champion earlier cultural manifestations of muscular Christianity start to sound a bit like schoolyard bullies rather than enlightened intellectuals.

They are also reactionaries rather than conservatives. What they want is to preserve in amber a certain aesthetic form and spiritual stance, even after huge cultural changes have rendered those things obsolete. It is one thing to bemoan the postmodern world, with its relentless consumerism and its secular public square, but it is quite another thing to blame artists for reflecting the times.

There is no way back. You can only move forward, which means that writers and artists have to begin with the way we live now and to somehow find in that unheroic, weekday world the whispers of grace. If people are alienated from authority, ignorant of the richness of their faith tradition, betrayed by religious leaders—if they are lost, wounded, resentful, and doubtful—then those stories have to be told, from the inside out. Genuine doubt is not weakness but strength, a willingness to wrestle with the angel.

Are there some writers and artists who use doubt and ambiguity as a way of dodging what T. S. Eliot called the "Overwhelming Question"? Sure. But the decline-and-fall critics are so sure of themselves that they don't bother to carefully sift what's out there. If they did, they'd find more kinship between the whisperers and the shouters than they have imagined.

Artists of faith may work on smaller canvases today, but if they can create exquisite miniatures, then they have done their bit to redeem the time.

Fully Human

Last night i watched—mesmerized, despite its near three-hour length—Andrei Tarkovsky's film *Stalker*, a minimalist science fiction epic set in a dreary, bombed-out industrial wasteland. The title does not derive from the contemporary connotation of the sexual predator, but goes back to the sort of guide who leads hunters to where game can be found. In fact, the script deliberately associates its stalker with the James Fenimore Cooper character Natty Bumppo, who is known as "Deerstalker."

In the film the stalker leads people into the Zone, a heavily fortified area guarded by machine-gun nests and roving patrols. Some years back, it seems, something—meteorite or spaceship—crashed there, leaving a device known as the Room, which apparently grants the wishes of those who enter it. There are those willing to try to get past the perimeter, but for this they need a stalker. The stalker's services are required not only because the authorities have sealed off the Zone but because the site has strange distortions of space and time, making any direct approach to the mysterious room impossible. Since Tarkovsky provides almost no exposition, some of these details have to be pieced together. But it helps to explain strange little gestures, such as the stalker's habit of tying bits of metal to pieces of cloth and tossing them ahead, as if to test for anomalies in the space-time continuum.

On this particular journey the stalker leads two men into the Zone; he calls them Professor and Writer, and they come to represent two distinct ways of looking at the world, that of science and art. The professor ostensibly wants to win the Nobel Prize (or at least gain the recognition of his colleagues) while the writer seeks inspiration. But the stalker reminds them that the Room grants only one's innermost wishes, and soon deeper, more complex motives begin to emerge. So do fears and defenses: one of the men is carrying a gun while the other has a suicide pill.

One might be tempted to idealize the stalker, but throughout the film he is an abject character, anxious and divided. Like Natty Bumppo, he is more at home in the Zone—a lush, wet, green place, despite the litter and waste that mar it—than in the gray world of the city. His daughter has been maimed by something he has picked up while in the Zone, and his wife suffers through his absences. Not everyone who ventures into the Zone survives, and that includes stalkers.

But for all his anxiety and suffering, the stalker possesses a kind of reverence for his task. He is a beggar, a suppliant, before a mystery. The professor calls him, somewhat scornfully, "God's fool," a term that had great resonance in the Russian culture Tarkovsky inherited and contains echoes of Dostoevsky's *The Brothers Karamazov,* with its own holy fool, Alyosha. At one point in the journey, as the stalker approaches a deep pool, he utters something like a prayer:

> May everything come true. May they believe. May they laugh at their passions. For that which they call passion is not really the energy of the soul, but merely friction between the soul and the outer world. But mostly may they have hope and may they become as helpless as children. For weakness is great and strength is worthless.

Of course, Andrei Tarkovsky was shaped by the experience of living under Soviet totalitarianism, which attempted to outlaw religious faith, so the professor and writer represent to him the failure of the two noblest human enterprises left to him—reason and imagination—while the stalker takes on religious connotations. If Tarkovsky had lived long enough to contemplate a remake of his own film, he might have added a fourth figure—the religious fanatic—to his band of pilgrims. Honesty compels the admission that ideological religion itself has emerged in a particularly fearsome way as one of the new forms of alienation from, and disdain for, mystery—and not merely in the Islamic world.

As I reflect this morning on the past two decades of publishing *Image,* I'd like to believe that this journal has been a place hospitable to contemporary stalkers, to those who throw probes out toward the mystery, those who know that to approach mystery is a long, arduous pilgrimage, best undertaken by those who know themselves to be beggars and fools.

Image was founded because the professor, the writer, and the fanatic are too much with us. Reason, imagination, and faith have gone their own ways, and the fragmentations and distortions that follow in the wake of that dreadful separation continue to haunt us. Without all three of these capacities we are less than fully human.

The path toward reintegration will require its own lengthy journey, because the interests surrounding these warring fiefdoms are powerful and entrenched. Nonetheless, many people do not feel represented by any of them and are in search of their own Zone. Many carry scars from past experiences, often inflicted by religion, making the road that much longer.

Paul Elie, author of *The Life You Save May Be Your Own*, a group biography about Dorothy Day, Flannery O'Connor, Thomas Merton, and Walker Percy, took up this subject in a recent essay in *Commonweal*. Though Elie wrote about the state of Catholic literature, his essay resonates beyond denominational boundaries. He praises O'Connor's insight into the postmodern world—its sense of displacement and uncertainty—but points out that her confidence in Church teaching as a countervailing force is precisely what contemporary writers lack, even writers who consider themselves to be believers.

To shed light on the present Elie employs a distinction made by the Victorian Matthew Arnold between a creative age and a critical one. Elie sees the era of O'Connor and the other three figures as a creative age, energized by modern secularism but confident in its faith. With the tremendous cultural shifts that took place in the 1960s and '70s, he believes we entered a critical age, characterized not by O'Connor's self-described mission "to make belief believable" but by skepticism—by the need to step back and, in Arnold's words, "to see the object as in itself it really is." The religious writer in a critical age starts from her own problems with the church, and her scrutiny can be anguished and harsh.

Elie is deeply sympathetic with the predicament of such writers, yet he is uncomfortable with the critical sensibility. His conclusion is bleak. Arguing that intransigent Church authorities are making the problem worse, he blames them for causing these writers to doubt the existence of God. He says that the current critical age is coming to an end, yet he is unsure whether a creative age will follow. We are living, he says, in a state of arrested development, the artist of faith paralyzed by Vatican pronouncements. Perhaps he thinks we're in Limbo.

While I have profound respect for Elie's many gifts, I cannot agree with his conclusions, and I believe the last twenty years of *Image* journal contain much of the evidence I need to make my case. In an earlier editorial in these pages I made my own distinction between religious writers of

O'Connor's generation and our own. Alluding to O'Connor's statement that "for the hard of hearing you have to shout," I contrasted "shouts" with the "whispers" of the current generation of writers. It is possible to be nostalgic for shouts, as many of my conservative friends are, but for a religious tradition based on the wisdom of the "still, small voice" I think it unwise to say that one mode is clearly better than the other.

Appealing as big concepts like "creative" and "critical" ages may be, they tend to break down under examination. Both impulses are at work at any given time; both are necessary for a healthy culture—or church, for that matter.

One of the editorial policies *Image* has followed from the beginning is the belief that our pages should contain both artists and writers who are grounded in faith communities and those who remain outside. Moreover, we've been interested in work that seems to us to grapple with religious questions even when their makers profess no faith at all.

This hasn't always been the easiest course to steer. Some would like *Image* to become little more than a highbrow outpost of the culture wars. And I suspect that certain artists have refrained from contributing to our pages because they fear being co-opted into a community that makes them uneasy.

Image is not a thesis-driven publication, unless creating a space for a perennial set of questions—stalkings, as it were—constitutes a thesis. That is also why we have refrained from backing a single artistic style as salvific—or a particular political agenda or religious subculture. After twenty years, it can be argued that the sheer diversity of work that *Image* has published demonstrates the persistence of the religious sense among those who make art—an ongoing struggle to integrate faith, reason, and imagination.

Elie is right to point out that many "critical" writers have turned to nonfiction to work out their agonistic relationship to church and belief. But he misses the most prominent themes of this nonfiction writing: stories of recovered faith, faith clung to despite the odds, and new conversion stories. What makes these narratives so compelling is that they are hard won, precisely because they seek to "see the object as in itself it really is." Needless to say, our pages have shown this to be true of all the art forms.

Where the editors of *Image* have come close to a thesis is our conviction that the effort to be fully human cannot ultimately be undertaken in solitude. Though there are many forces in our culture that lead us, willingly or unwillingly, to reduce religion to a merely private experience—to "spirituality"—this is to rob it of meaning and to surrender to solipsism. We believe that the Jewish and Christian roots of our culture, though tainted by terrible sins of omission and commission, can and should be renewed by reason and imagination. As any artist should know, you cannot have content without a form. To reject institutions, to refuse to reform them and be formed by them, is a counsel of despair.

In the two decades that *Image* has been publishing, the gatekeepers of culture have become less aggressively secular, but the myth that enduring art inspired by faith is a thing of the past has not gone out of circulation. It is still possible for a reviewer in the *New Republic* to write: "the absence of God from our literature feels so normal, so self-evident, that one realizes with a shock how complete it is." That is the sort of blinkered view that occurs when people begin to believe their own propaganda.

In Tarkovsky's film the professor and the writer are not held up for vilification; they speak for pathways to truth that we can never abandon. They may enter the Zone with mixed motives, but they go anyway. Whatever their heads may tell them, their hearts' desire is to draw close to mystery. The religious sense is part of what it means to be fully human. *Image* will continue to present the best writing and art that speak to this ineradicable desire of the human heart.

FAITH SPEAKS TO ART

Thirty Seconds Away

The following is an expanded version of the introductory remarks delivered at Image's *Glen Workshop in Santa Fe, New Mexico, on July 27, 2009. The theme for both the workshop and* Image's *twentieth anniversary year, now concluding, was "Fully Human: Art and the Religious Sense."*

BY ALL ACCOUNTS, SAINT Irenaeus of Lyons, a bishop of the early church, didn't have it easy. For one thing, he'd left the thriving, well-established Christian community in Asia Minor for what was, in essence, missionary territory. Lyons was hardly the back of the beyond—it was, in fact, a thriving commercial center in southern Gaul that did a lot of trade with the East, which was why Christianity could slip in so easily. But if the bourgeois cosmopolitanism of the city offered opportunities for the fledgling church, it also posed its own set of challenges.

Irenaeus found himself dividing his time between spreading the gospel, helping his community endure the waves of brutal persecution that came as the mood struck various Roman emperors, and responding to the competition—the exotic cults and religious fads that might be thought of as the Roman Empire's equivalent of the New Age.

Things had been rather different back home. There the church already had a history. Born in the first half of the second century, Irenaeus had, as a young man, listened to the preaching of the renowned bishop of Smyrna, Saint Polycarp. Polycarp was already an old man by that time; he had been a disciple of Saint John the Evangelist, who had known the Lord. (Polycarp was eventually burned at the stake—and it is possible that Irenaeus also died a martyr's death.)

Imagine the young bishop struggling to build a church in the bustling city of Lyons, just after the latest persecution had taken several dozen members of his community. If ever a person had the right to feel embattled and pessimistic, consumed by a sense of futility and the darkness of human nature, it was Irenaeus.

But in his famous treatise *Against the Heretics,* written in the year 185, Irenaeus uttered these astonishing words: *Gloria Dei vivens homo.*

"The glory of God is man fully alive." This sentence has haunted me ever since I heard it many years ago.

What does it mean? Irenaeus wrote those words in response to one of the other popular cults of the time, Gnosticism. The Gnostics held that the created order—matter itself—was evil, and that salvation could only come through a secret knowledge of how to escape into a purely spiritual realm. The Gnostics tended to assert that Jesus was not fully incarnate as a human being but something more like a ghostly projection—like the hologram of Princess Leia in the first *Star Wars* movie.

Distant and alien as the Gnostics may appear to modern sensibilities, their way of thinking has a familiar ring. They tended to split into two camps: those who became dissolute libertines—why not indulge this flesh from which we will eventually escape?—and hyper-moralistic ascetics who forbade marriage and sexual intercourse and ate only the blandest foods.

Here it is possible to feel Irenaeus as our contemporary, because there are plenty of Gnostics left these days, whether of the hedonistic or moralistic sort. The modern cult of the supermodel manages to combine both strands into one: a highly sexualized body that is simultaneously anorexic.

This may sound odd, but I believe that the problem today isn't that people don't have a sufficient understanding of spirituality; it's that we don't understand our own humanity.

Perhaps that's why Irenaeus's belief that the glory of God is man fully alive sounds scandalous to our ears. Like the Gnostics, most of us tend to be pretty harsh on the subject of the human condition, whether we are religious believers or not.

We inherit a tradition that says we are made in the image and likeness of God, but we are not comfortable in our own skins. Or as Walker Percy used to put it, we don't coincide with ourselves.

For most of us, the discomfort is not so much with the big sins of violence and betrayal. What tend to get us down are the quotidian frustrations of our own embodiedness, and therefore of contingency, limitation, dependence, need. We are creatures driven by desire but so easily disappointed, even when we get what we think we want.

Which is where the gnostic temptation enters in. If the human condition is lost and alienated, then the alternative is to seek refuge in one aspect of our natures, and so we strive to become either beasts or angels—alternatives that our culture provides us in abundance.

Popular culture thrives by creating the myth of invulnerability—to time, the effects of aging on the body, financial insecurity, you name it.

Its goal is to create an immortal beast.

Religious culture often seeks the same sort of invulnerability, but from the opposite angle, asking us to live in the spiritual abstractions of apologetics and moralism, creating an ideological ghetto, a fortress impervious to doubt and ambiguity.

Its goal is to create mortal angels.

In Christian circles, the gnostic tendency is remarkably persistent; the realm of spirit is always elsewhere, beyond the circumstances of the human condition. And so you hear believers speaking earnestly about why we should be wishing for "the world as it ought to be."

While I respect the intentions behind this sort of thinking, I find it misguided. There is some value in pointing out the disparity between what we are capable of being and what we actually are, but the danger of this mentality is that it leads us away from the essential truth of our embodied, contingent selves, toward some ethereal realm outside our present experience. Gnosticism has a way of sneaking in the back door.

But what if these conditions are, in the end, gifts—the very means by which we become fully alive? What if grace enters in and through these limitations? What if this is what Irenaeus was getting at? The religious sense, inherent in human nature, grows out of the awareness of our dependence; it is marked by an intuition that existence itself is a gift and that the proper response to it is wonder. Luigi Giussani once made the disconcerting claim that "the beggar is the protagonist of history," an assertion that probably won't be found in too many textbooks. But it has an oddly compelling logic and brings to mind the image of Saint Francis, wallowing in the dirt, ecstatic and free. There was a man who coincided with himself.

What we need is not the notion of a world that ought to be but the capacity to see the dimension of grace irradiating the world that *is*. It seems to me that if we are to be redeemed, it must be in and through the way we *are*.

A few years ago a holy priest from Italy was on a visit to the American southwest and had to pass through Las Vegas on his way to a retreat in the desert. When his hosts showed him, with no little trepidation, the bizarre panoply of greed, vanity, and fantasy upon which the city rests (a city that Saint Irenaeus would have recognized and understood), he had one simple response.

"My God," he said, "these people are all thirty seconds away from salvation."

I think he is right. Our humanity—the human heart—is constituted by certain elementary needs—for happiness, justice, beauty. The tired old Christian approach of moralistic condemnation of the wrong pathways to the satisfaction of these needs misses the point.

What we need to see is the inherent religious sense in human beings; we need to awaken the connection between desire and its home in God. Nor, except in the rarest of cases—and here I'm thinking of certain mystics—can that pathway to God be found except in and through "the things of this world."

In order to refute the Gnostics, Irenaeus had to prove that God himself chose to accept the limits and contingencies of a human life. The Gnostics, rejecting embodiment, relegate God to a sphere beyond the created order, which only those with esoteric knowledge can discover. But for Irenaeus this is a fatal rejection of the world and our place in it. The words that follow his statement that the glory of God is man fully alive are: "and the life of man consists in beholding God."

To demonstrate that our beholding of God is not like watching a hologram, Irenaeus goes back to Genesis. When Moses encounters God on the mountain top, Irenaeus notes, he is told to plant himself within a cleft in the rock. While Moses is rooted there, God will allow him to see his "back parts." Using a richly metaphorical form of biblical interpretation, Irenaeus sees that cleft in the rock as symbolic of the human condition itself. Moses is granted only a partial view, but in the incarnation, Christ himself enters the cleft of the rock. "Through the wisdom of God," Irenaeus writes, "man shall see him . . . in the depth of a rock, that is, in his coming as a man."

The bishop of Lyons may not have considered the Bible a work of literature, but his method is profoundly literary. Which is why we might say that writers and artists are uniquely situated to help us achieve the perception of grace within contingency.

The film director Akira Kurosawa said that the "artist is the one who does not look away." The artist maintains her gaze at human neediness and dependency, and through the honesty and beauty of the form she creates, enables us to connect that need with its true source and lasting fulfillment.

The artist works in an incarnational medium, profoundly aware of contingency and embodiedness. And yet art's very greatness is the way that it can adumbrate the presence of grace in and through the messiness of our lives.

If this is not true, then the doctrine of the incarnation is meaningless.

This is another place where gnosticism creeps in. We don't look at the incarnation rightly. We see it as the divine descending, perhaps condescending, to the human level—as if Jesus had to hold his nose while taking human form.

The church fathers, including Irenaeus, did not see it that way. According to the ancient and authoritative Athanasian Creed, Christ's incarnation means that human and divine are "One, not by conversion of the Godhead into flesh, but by taking of the Manhood into God."

In short, to paraphrase the art historian Hans Rookmaaker, "Christ did not come to make us Christians; he came to make us human beings."

The artist does not show us the world as it ought to be; she shows us the world as it is, here and now, and enables us to see that our redemption is always present, always available. It is not a message to be communicated but a presence and a mystery to be experienced—in the flesh. Art, as a fleshly medium, is one place where presence and mystery can be encountered and received.

We are all thirty seconds away from salvation.

Religious but Not Spiritual

FOR A NUMBER OF years I've been saving up the fiction of Anthony Trollope as a sort of mid-life treat. At least I hoped it would be a treat. Trollope is the kind of author who is often ridiculed as a literary lightweight: a Victorian lacking the range and energy of Dickens; a drawing-room chronicler without Jane Austen's tart irony or powers of observation. Even as I turned to the first page I was braced for disappointment.

So far I can report that Trollope—for all his gentle romantic farce and clerical satire—stands up quite well as a distinctive literary voice, capable of striking deep social and political resonances upon the gossamer strings of his comedy. While the pages go down easily, Trollope is not merely a fashioner of escapist fluff but a writer who summons issues as profound as those his more earnest contemporaries wrestled with.

I began with *The Warden,* the first in a sequence known as *The Chronicles of Barsetshire* (which includes most famously *Barchester Towers*). The title refers to the novel's protagonist, the Reverend Septimus Harding, a clergyman nearing sixty who lives in a sleepy English shire where time seems to pass more slowly than in the great metropolis of London. No one in the town of Barchester is more happily attuned to this timelessness and obscurity than the good reverend. But to his horror he suddenly finds himself at the center of national attention.

As precentor of Barchester Cathedral, Harding is also given the wardenship of Hiram's Hospital, an almshouse for elderly or disabled working men. Like many such institutions, this almshouse was founded by a local worthy in the Middle Ages. The income from the donated properties has increased substantially over the centuries and is largely given to the warden. Thanks to the efforts of a well-intentioned, young, reform-minded doctor, John Bold (who happens to be in love with Harding's daughter), the Reverend Harding and Hiram's Hospital become a *cause célèbre,* the subject of newspaper articles about social inequality and the power of the Church of England.

On one level *The Warden* is about the human toll inflicted on good people by crusading reformers intent on winning points on the political stage. The Reverend Harding, while never particularly guilty about the eight hundred pounds he received as warden, sees the point of the critique. Because Trollope always wanted to depict his characters as mixtures of good and bad he shows us a man who resigns his position (against the wishes of his clerical colleagues) as much because of an aversion to publicity as from a newly awakened conscience about social justice.

But if that was all the book was about I don't think *The Warden* would be as beloved as it is. What makes the story special is that while Harding's weaknesses are clear—he is an excessively shy, retiring person who may not act or think for himself as he should—nonetheless, he participates in an ancient, organic union of faith and community that stretches back into the medieval world that produced Hiram's Hospital.

Trollope takes care to give the Reverend Harding a highly specific role within the church: he is a liturgist and choirmaster. Early in the novel we are given an economical introduction to Harding's passions:

> Mr. Harding's warmest admirers cannot say that he was ever an industrious man; the circumstances of his life have not called on him to be so; and yet he can hardly be called an idler. Since his appointment to his precentorship, he has published, with all possible additions of vellum, typography, and gilding, a collection of our ancient church music, with some correct dissertations on Purcell, Crotch, and Nares. He has greatly improved the choir of Barchester, which, under his dominion, now rivals that of any cathedral in England. He has taken something more than his fair share in the cathedral services, and has played the violoncello daily to such audiences as he could collect, or, *faute de mieux,* to no audience at all.

The small touches here are delightful—and telling. That book of ancient church music is published so beautifully, it turns out, at Harding's personal expense, much to the exasperation of his son-in-law, the Reverend Theophilus Grantly, the officious and money-conscious archdeacon of Barchester Cathedral. It is perhaps the warden's only extravagance but it is clearly an extravagance of love and a celebration of beauty. Harding's passion for the cello, which later in the novel is described as "that saddest of instruments," is manifest whenever he is emotionally overwrought; at such times he is given to silently "bowing" a passage of music, much to the consternation of his interlocutors.

Harding's faith is played out in the minutiae of liturgy and music rather than the grand thoughts of preaching and theological exposition. His other gift is simply that of friendship. Significantly, his two deepest relationships are with the bishop and the de facto leader of the Hiram's Hospital community, a simple old soul named Bunce—two men who represent the top and bottom of the social order. Harding and his bishop love to spend companionable evenings by the fire. As for Bunce: "The precentor delighted to call him his sub-warden, and was not ashamed, occasionally, when no other guest was there, to bid him sit down by the same parlor fire, and drink the full glass of port which was placed near him. Bunce never went without the second glass, but no entreaty ever made him take a third."

Trollope's observations about his characters are generous but rarely sentimental, as that small detail of class consciousness ("when no other guest was there") makes clear. Septimus Harding lives in what essentially remains a feudal world, and if that dispensation is both static and guilty of certain inequities, the new world of the reformers has little of its warmth and humanity, its rootedness in a historic community.

The high-minded idealism of activists like John Bold, for all its rhetoric of compassion and equality, does not grow out of direct contact with the poor. Its motives are thoroughly mixed. Good intentions shade into personal vanity; lofty (if vague) goals for the reform of allegedly corrupt institutions are quickly exploited by newspapers that profit from controversy. Neither the reformers nor the media have any real stake in the ongoing life of this community.

And a bewildered Septimus Harding is reduced to playing melancholy notes on his air cello.

I read *The Warden* at a time when I was reflecting on the now ubiquitous contemporary phrase: "I'm spiritual but not religious." I asked a friend about this phrase and he replied: "Many associate the word *religious* with fanaticism, irrationality, intolerance, and closed-mindedness, while *spirituality* suggests something more detached, thoughtful, tolerant, and open." The "binding" (*re-ligare*) of religion is seen as overly constrictive.

No doubt this is an accurate assessment of a widespread feeling. And yet—call me contrary or misguided if you will—the Reverend Harding makes me think that I'm religious but not spiritual.

Communities, like families, can be healthy or toxic, but Western individualism provides no true alternative. Ironically, the spiritual-but-not-religious embrace a consumerist mentality that in other contexts they harshly criticize. The irony is compounded when one realizes that these spiritual individualists—inheritors of an "I" culture—most often pluck items off the shelf of "we" cultures. Spiritual tourism offers the benefits of wisdom derived from those who submit to authority and discipline and tradition without having to do so oneself.

But spiritual tourists have no home to return to; they are always restlessly consuming new experiences. They can't eat, pray, and love enough.

At the level of popular culture the tremendous longing we feel for the integrated life of a "we" culture is overwhelmingly clear. Take a film like *Avatar,* which presents us with a thinly veiled allegory of rapacious consumerism confronted by a seemingly primitive tribal culture that is grounded in taboos, strict social roles, and corporate worship. The bulldozers that plow through the jungle seek to rip out a precious piece of the whole and turn it into a commodity.

The mid-twentieth-century theologian Romano Guardini noted that his conversion experience began with the spiritual desire to "lose his life in order to find it." At that moment he ran into a dilemma:

> To give my soul away—but to whom? Who is in the position to require it from me? So to require it that, in the requiring, it would not again be I who lay hold of it? Not simply "God." For whenever a person wants to deal only with God, then he says "God" but means himself. There must also be an objective authority, which can draw out my answer from self-assertion's every refuge and hideout. But there is only one such entity: the . . . church in her authority and concreteness. The question of holding on or letting go is decided ultimately not before God, but before the church.

The word *authority* is another contemporary bugbear, I know, but in the end, authority as Guardini sees it is less about someone handing down judgments from on high upon hapless members and more about the force that compels us to stick together. God knows just how hard and messy that sticking can be.

How, I wonder, is it possible to learn tolerance *outside* of a community?

The older I get the more suspicious I am of spirituality as something ethereal, exotic, and otherworldly—something found elsewhere. The poet William Carlos Williams coined the phrase "No ideas but in things" to express a poetic that preferred concreteness to abstraction. By the same token, I know of no spirituality outside the relationships that constitute the daily life of my community.

This is where Trollope's genius lies in *The Warden*. For in making Septimus Harding a liturgist he emphasizes that the quintessential activity of a religious community is not the purveying of doctrines and ideas but the worship of the presence that has called the community into being. In common prayer and song we lay aside the burden of self-consciousness; we recount the story of the encounter that brought us together. In worship we become participants, living members of a body, rather than observers and connoisseurs.

Liturgy is where art and community life meet. Where spirit is not thought but made flesh through hands, knees, and vocal cords. In worship the stuff of art is offered up in the name of the community, not the ego of the artist—or the clergy. Ingmar Bergman, one of the great film directors and an artist capable of rendering dysfunctional religious communities with unrelenting, devastating accuracy, nonetheless wrote late in his life: "Art lost its basic creative drive the moment it was separated from worship. It severed an umbilical cord and now lives its own sterile life, generating and degenerating itself. In former days the artist remained unknown and his work was to the glory of God."

After Septimus Harding resigns his wardenship of Hiram's Hospital he is assigned to the tiny church of Saint Cuthbert, "no bigger than an ordinary room." "Here he performs afternoon service every Sunday, and administers the sacrament once in every three months. His audience is not large . . . but enough come to fill his six pews, and on the front seat of those devoted to the poor is always to be seen our old friend Mr. Bunce, decently arrayed in his bedesman's gown."

My kind of place.

Current Event

HE SAID HE NEVER intended to found anything, and I believe him. But he had a gift for friendship. When his funeral mass was celebrated in Milan last month, 30,000 of his companions were there. The principal celebrant, Cardinal Ratzinger, read a message from another friend, Karol Wojtyla.

It may be a truism to say that every saint is a saint for his times, but in the case of Father Luigi Giussani, the match between charism—the particular form of faith he felt called to live—and the spirit of the age was nothing short of extraordinary. In the early 1950s, he sensed a widening gap between traditional religious institutions and the daily emotional life of the people. He saw the turmoil and restlessness beneath the good times, the growing polarization of radicals and reactionaries, the steady drift toward the utopian politics of revolution or retrenchment.

Giussani perceived these forces working within the religious community as well, leading many to a faith that was increasingly abstract and moralistic. It might seem odd that a Catholic priest would criticize moralism, but he did, whether it was at work in the language of traditionalist piety or the slogans of political activism. Giussani said that the essence of faith is neither doctrine nor morality, but something else, something far more fundamental. Of his own tradition he wrote: "Christianity is an event. There is no other word to indicate its nature: neither the word *law* nor the word *ideology, conception,* or *project*. Christianity is not a religious doctrine, a series of moral laws, a complex of rites. Christianity is a fact, an event: everything else is a consequence."

What sort of event was it? An encounter, Giussani said, something that might be described as a chance meeting. He knew that people might object to the word *chance*, associating it with randomness, but he pointed out that the ancient philosophers had thought of chance as "an effect greater than the sum of its known causes." In short, chance favors the prepared mind.

Some of the most important moments of our lives take this form: an event appears random, but mysteriously unlocks something that has been dormant, unrealized, within us. In that sort of encounter we experience something utterly new and unique: what we meet corresponds to the deepest desires of our hearts.

What set Giussani apart from so many religious leaders is that he believed the encounter with God does not annul our humanity, lifting us into the ether, but restores us to ourselves. He was fond of quoting the ancient Roman rhetor, Marius Victorinus, who said: "When I encountered Christ, I discovered I was a man."

I first encountered Giussani when I chanced upon a book of his entitled *Morality: Memory and Desire*. It was the subtitle that got me: not only the allusion to the phrase from T. S. Eliot's *The Waste Land,* but a sudden intuition that these two words might make sense of a subject that has been reduced, time and time again, to banality. In the book Giussani writes that morality is less a set of abstract principles or laws than a way of honoring a relationship. The essence of the Way lies in the companionship of those who live in memory of the Event.

A few years later I attended a retreat held by the Catholic lay movement Giussani founded: Communion and Liberation. After a day of spiritual meditations, the evening was devoted to a party. Because the movement was only just beginning in the United States, there were a lot of Italians in the room that night. The air was thick with cigarette smoke and the wine was plentiful. A pianist and a saxophonist were jamming somewhere in the blue haze. I think the cluster of people I was with were discussing the films of Andrei Tarkovsky. Then, late that evening, one of the elders of the group—he must have been all of thirty-five—stood up and announced that it was time to go to bed. Within seconds, the entire group was chanting the *Salve Regina* in hushed unison. The party was over . . . until the following evening.

For an American like me, used to thinking that religion involved segmenting my life into sacred and profane compartments, the experience was disconcerting and, well, liberating. I suspected that national character had something to do with it, but there was also something else at work, a spirit of freedom that I had not felt before.

Shortly before he died, Giussani was quoted as saying that he had never intended to found anything. It all began in 1954, when he was a young seminary professor. A few chance conversations about faith with young people had profoundly disturbed him. He sensed both anger and ignorance, a widespread feeling that religion had little to do with life, and a tendency to displace faith with dreams of political utopia. So he made a fateful decision: he left his comfortable seminary position to teach high school religion classes.

When he entered the classroom, instead of giving his students predigested bits of Thomas Aquinas, he read the poetry of the dark, despairing, Romantic Giacomo Leopardi with them. They spoke of the poet's unfulfilled desires, his sadness and sense of mystery. And then he would ask them to consider Aquinas's belief that this sadness might be "the desire for an absent good." And so a companionship began.

In his funeral homily, Cardinal Ratzinger said of Giussani: "from the start [of his life] he was touched—or, better—wounded, by the desire for beauty." He believed that art provides the best analogy for the moment of recognition that is our experience of the Event. The spiritual life, he said, is "the development of a gaze."

In a documentary made before his death, Giussani's voice is hoarse, and he looks down while speaking. But when he finishes his sentence and looks up, you see a gaze that might make you a friend for life.

East and West in Miniature

THE RECENT CONTROVERSY OVER Pope Benedict XVI's Regensburg lecture—which touched on the nature of human reason, but which also questioned, in passing, the relationship between faith and reason in Islam—may turn out to be more productive than was at first thought. Among other things, it generated a substantive open letter to the pope signed by thirty-eight respected Muslim clerics—a document that itself is carefully reasoned and gracious. At a time when the rising tide of Islamic fundamentalism and terrorism is being met by increasing fear and stereotyping in the West, any form of dialogue is cause for hope.

In his insightful essay "The Dialogue with Islam," Stratford Caldecott points out that a classic Western concern about Islam is that it seems to stress the absolute will of Allah without a corresponding emphasis on how that will manifests a reasonable, ordered universe. A religion founded on mere will, of course, would make dialogue irrelevant and provide an endless fuel supply for violent conflict. What makes Caldecott's essay so fresh and provocative is not the evidence he provides for an Islamic tradition of reason (though he does believe it exists), but the suggestion that a more fruitful avenue for dialogue with Islam would be the investigation not of reason but of beauty.

Over the centuries, as Caldecott notes, one of the central strands of Islam has been what is known as the "*ihsani* tradition." The Arabic word *ihsan* derives from the noun *hasana*, which means to be beautiful, good, lovely. As a verb, *ihsan* means to "make beautiful or good." According to scholar Joseph Lumbard, God himself is the first to make beautiful. Thus the Prophet Muhammad prays: "O God, you have made beautiful my creation (*khalq*), make beautiful my character (*khuluq*)." Lumbard argues that the process by which one becomes beautiful is less a rationalistic or legalistic thing than it is the cultivation of a craft or art form. The great Sufi scholars, poets, and mystics stressed that *ihsan* involved the cultivation of inner discipline.

Nowhere are the issues of Islam, beauty, and cultural/religious conflict more meaningfully explored than in the novel *My Name Is Red*, by Orhan Pamuk, the Turkish writer awarded the 2006 Nobel Prize for Literature. Written prior to 9/11, this novel explores another time and place dominated by a volatile clash of civilizations: late-sixteenth-century Istanbul, where the Ottoman Empire was engaged in incessant conflict both within and without.

Pamuk's attraction to this "distant mirror" stems directly from his own personal history. Born into a well-to-do family, Pamuk grew up in a westernized neighborhood of Istanbul. He studied art, architecture, and journalism—as well as creative writing at the Iowa Writers' Workshop—but never pursued them professionally. After completing his education, he decided to devote himself entirely to writing, something his family's financial position enabled him to do.

One of the overriding themes of Pamuk's novels is the ambiguity of Turkish identity, the fate of a country situated at the crossroads between Europe and Asia. For centuries Turks have struggled with the self-consciousness of a people who believe they are imitators. The anguished search for authenticity leads some to seek a lost purity, as in the case of Islamic fundamentalism.

My Name Is Red is a sprawling, intricately plotted, multiply narrated tale, centering around a workshop boasting the Empire's greatest manuscript illuminators. The tradition of illuminated "miniatures," already ancient by the time the novel takes place, had reached its apex in the great Persian masters of the medieval era. But the tradition was fed by many contributing streams, including those from as far east as China and Mongolia. In the wisdom of the religious authorities, the Islamic prohibition against representational art was not applied to illuminations because they were considered extensions and embellishments of the manuscripts they enhanced. The texts might include works of literature—those by Nizami and Ferdowsi haunt the narrative—or elaborate memorial books created especially for shahs and sultans.

The plot of Pamuk's novel is set into motion by two events: the brutal murder of one of the most famous illuminators, known by his nickname "Elegant," and the return to Istanbul after twelve years of a man called "Black." As it happens, Black was a member of the same workshop as Elegant, but had left when his suit for his beautiful cousin Shekure was rejected by his uncle Enishte, himself a master artist. Black's investigation into the murder and his renewed pursuit of Shekure drive the story forward.

In all, twelve narrators render various aspects of the story, including Elegant (from the afterlife); Esther, the Jewish cloth-seller (a *yenta* and go-between); the three greatest illuminators—Olive, Butterfly, and Stork; and the unnamed murderer himself. Another running feature of the novel involves monologues by things depicted in miniatures. The performance of these monologues is undertaken by a storyteller in a coffee shop frequented by illuminators; he sets up pictures and speaks as: a dog, a gold coin, two dervishes, a horse, death, Satan, and even the color red.

Like the greatest miniatures, *My Name Is Red* is a combination of motion and stasis, of intricate ornamentation and frenetic activity. But above all it is a profound meditation on the meaning of art and religion. Before long it becomes clear that a motive for the killing of Elegant is a project initiated by the sultan and entrusted to Enishte: the creation of a secret book, one that adopts the "Frankish" style of painting that has been brought to Istanbul by Venetian diplomats and merchants. The ostensible purpose of the volume is to demonstrate that the Ottoman Empire can outdo its Western rivals, but the project requires the artists to break a series of powerful taboos: rendering an individual portrait of the sultan, employing perspectival technique that might make a tree look bigger than a mosque, and the more elusive but nonetheless forbidden pursuit of a personal artistic style.

One might imagine that Pamuk the sophisticated contemporary novelist would, at this point in the narrative, tip the scales toward a modern, individualistic conception of art. But this he does not do. Throughout the course of the novel, the traditional view is portrayed with sympathy. To be sure, he does give us a sense of the puritanical strain when the murderer says to Enishte Effendi:

> On the Day of Judgment, the idol-makers will be asked to bring the images they created to life. Since they will be unable to bring anything to life, their lot will be to suffer the torments of Hell. Let it not be forgotten that in the Glorious Koran, "creator" is one of the attributes of God. It is Allah who is creative, who brings that which is not into existence, who gives life to the lifeless. No one ought to compete with Him. The greatest of sins is committed by painters who presume to do as He does, who claim to be as creative as He.

But alongside this heavily moralistic argument—the one we're all familiar with—Pamuk sees the beauty and the mysticism behind the ancient vision. The artist who serves Allah seeks the humble path of self-effacement and strives to render the timeless, eternal truth of creation. As an apophatic religion, Islam refrains from making analogies between Allah and the created order. And so it should come as no surprise that the crowning achievement of a lifetime's work for the Persian masters was blindness—the ultimate union with the uncreated creator. "Blindness is a realm of bliss from which the Devil and guilt are barred," the miniaturist called Olive says.

The intrusion of Western consciousness into this realm is truly shocking; it appears to be nothing less than blasphemy and pride. And yet there are those who share a glimmer of understanding. No less a figure than the sultan himself says to Enishte:

> If I believed, heaven forbid, the way these infidels do, that the Prophet Jesus was also the Lord God Himself, then I'd also hold that God could be observed in this world, and even, that he could manifest in human form; only then might I accept the depiction of mankind in full detail and exhibit such images.

Enishte represents the possibility of a cosmopolitan attitude. In response to the idea that the influence of Western art will contaminate the purity of miniature painting, Enishte replies that the entire tradition rests upon the mingling of Arabic illustrating sensibility and Mongol-Chinese painting. "Nothing is pure," he concludes. "To God belongs the East and the West."

Of course, *My Name Is Red* is itself an example of art as a hybrid of disparate visions. But merely to conclude that Pamuk has achieved a postmodern rendering of all points of view would be faint praise. John Updike has written that "Pamuk's ingenuity is yoked to a profound sense of enigma and doubleness." The capacity for doubleness allows him to render the alienation of those caught between religious and cultural traditions, but it can also do justice to the virtues of each tradition. The overwhelming conviction on finishing *My Name Is Red* is precisely how art can represent the *ihsani* vision of "making beautiful."

The tradition of miniature painting came to an end soon after the events narrated in *My Name Is Red*, in part because of large-scale cultural and political forces that dried up the sources of its creativity. In times of conflict, pragmatism and puritanism, however opposed to one another, combine to put an end to art.

But this novel does not suggest that artists are mere victims. Pamuk believes that the making of art has moral implications. Art is not a privileged realm: the painstaking disciplines that lead to mastery may also lead to vanity and pride. By the end of *My Name Is Red* it is difficult to avoid the conclusion that artists themselves can be partly responsible for the end of art. The same thought could be applied to both the artists and the political leaders of the West, where individualism has led to the ills that many in the Islamic world want no part of.

While Pamuk is not a religious man, the integrity of his "doubleness" enables him to honor the moral concerns that religion evokes. He is a unquestionably a master, but he knows that "making beautiful" also requires "doing beautiful." For this reason, it should be clear that beauty is opposed to mere will, that it reflects an awareness of the intricacy and order of creation.

In the Koran, God is known under ninety-nine names, one of which is Beauty. That may be the best place for dialogue between cultures and religions to begin.

Picturing the Passion

Now that Mel Gibson's *The Passion of the Christ* has reached thousands of screens around the world and the frenzy of editorializing, pre- and post-release, has died down, two of the early questions about the film have been answered. Once the film entered the public domain, most of the fears about whether it was anti-Semitic dissipated, leaving only some concern about the possibility that in certain parts of the globe anti-Semites might use the film to incite violence. The other question—would *The Passion's* graphic violence keep people away from the theaters—has been answered with a resounding no. The numbers are such that any attempt to characterize interest in the film as mere curiosity strikes me as strained. Indeed, the controversy over Gibson's film has become something of a mirror image of the earlier culture war shouting match over Martin Scorsese's *The Last Temptation of Christ*: in the case of the present film, it is the critics who have turned up their noses and the public who have filled the theaters.

I was prepared to dislike this film. Having had a few unpleasant run-ins over the years with hyper-traditionalist Catholicism at its most ideological and eccentric, and hearing that Gibson might have a similar world view, I was ready to seize upon any sign of anti-Semitism, esoteric religious symbolism, or political paranoia. What I encountered was something far more centric, more deeply grounded in the aesthetic and theological traditions of Christianity than I had expected. Disturbing and emotionally draining as *The Passion* may be, it is a remarkable achievement, a daring recovery of iconographic and theological language that had all but disappeared from the public realm.

That the film has its share of flaws and misjudgments I will readily grant. For example, there is the fundamental difficulty of translating the words of the Bible into a different medium. The history of film is strewn with abject failures in this genre, large and small. A few years ago the writer Virginia Stem Owens touched on this issue in a book review of Frederick

Buechner's novel, *The Son of Laughter*, which recounts some of the Genesis narrative from Isaac's point of view. In the review, Owens quotes from Erich Auerbach's classic work, *Mimesis*, to make her point:

> *The Son of Laughter* definitely succeeds in terms of entertainment and passionate narrative. Yet, like other novels borrowing from biblical stories, it simply fills in too much, closing the gaps which, Auerbach says, are intended "to overcome our reality." Any reality we add will always be exasperatingly partial. Instead of explaining the biblical world in our terms, we must "fit our own life into its world" and allow ourselves "to be elements in its structure of universal history." The gaps are meant to swallow us.

A director of consummate artistry like Wim Wenders would probably endorse the point Owens made. For someone like Wenders, the frontal approach is doomed to failure: better to refract the ancient story in oblique ways through contemporary narratives that give us situations and characters to which we can relate. The invisible reality of faith is something best made visible when it haunts the edges of consciousness and memory.

However compelling these points may be, it would be obtuse not to recognize that there is a fundamental human need to reimagine the ancient stories in whatever media are available. In the smorgasbord of aesthetic choices, there will always be a corner of the table for more direct approaches, however fraught with risk they may be.

Gibson's use of sustained, graphic violence in *The Passion* is another gamble that many people have questioned. Even a sympathetic Christian viewer like theologian Gil Bailie feels that Gibson miscalculated here. The danger of this level of violence is that it will turn Jesus into the gold medalist in the Olympics of Suffering. Bailie writes:

> Christ's death changed the human condition forever, not because he suffered more than anyone else ever did, but because, as "the Lamb slain from the foundation of the world," he suffered the fate of every victim everywhere. . . . The shocking thing about the cross of Christ is that God's Anointed One dies on it, revealing once and for all the otherwise unimaginable truth about the depths of God's love.

It is at this juncture where one bumps up against the limits of even the best acting and cinematography. Gibson does make an effort to have Jesus look at those around him with ever-deepening love and compassion as the passion progresses. But his film is far more effective in tracing the transformative effect of Christ's sacrifice on bystanders like Simon of Cyrene and the centurion, and on the two Marys, than he is able to convey divinity through his protagonist.

Ultimately, the strongest defense for the use of violence in this film is the issue of sacramentality, the Christian belief that the incarnation hallows our human, corporeal condition. In the history of the church, Christ is always being etherealized, rendered comfortably abstract, by liberals and conservatives. One of the enduring strengths of *The Passion* is its use of gesture, touch, and gaze to convey presence. Once again, it is the figure of Mary, superbly played by Maia Morgenstern, who conveys this most vividly. When, near the end of the film, Mary kisses her son's foot on the cross, her face is smeared with blood, as if she is drunk on wine—an allusion both to the wedding at Cana and the Eucharist.

Moments like this abound in the film, though they can be hard to retain in the midst of the engulfing horror. But they are there, from the hand of the fallen Magdalene inching across to the foot of her savior (both paralleling and opposing the snake that crawls toward him in Gethsemane) to Mary's homing movements as she hunkers on the ground above the place where her son is being held in the hellish womb of captivity below. When he is given his cross to bear, Jesus hugs it to himself like a man being reunited with his lover. Mary's willing embrace of Christ's suffering—the "Yes" that parallels the Annunciation—gives the film emotional and spiritual ballast.

Gibson's decision to introduce a number of supernatural elements into the story, including the figure of Satan (who does not appear in the Gospel accounts of the Passion), seems to be a crime against the very sacramentalism that otherwise gives the film its power. I wish he had kept the story relentlessly on the human plane, so that by focusing on the visible and tangible, the invisible would register there and there only.

The religion scholar Stephen Prothero has criticized what he calls Gibson's "blood and guts sacramentality." But what other kind is there? If God cannot become present in blood, guts, shit, piss, semen, saliva—he vanishes into the ether. In short, this is not the Messiah of the Jesus Seminar, who increasingly seems to resemble a divinity being graded on a curve. In his *New York Times* op-ed on the film, Kenneth Woodward aptly quoted the famous formula coined by theologian H. Richard Niebuhr to criticize the modern therapeutic vision of Christianity: "A God without wrath brought men without sin into a kingdom without judgment through the ministrations of a Christ without a cross."

Does *The Passion* represent an excessive reaction? Does it signal the resurgence of some sort of dark, atavistic religion? The return of a manly Christ as opposed to a more sensitive and inclusive savior? I'm not so sure. Gibson's Jesus puts me in mind of a column from a British newspaper that my wife once read out loud to me. In an article on the relationship between the sexes in the early 1980s, numerous women were quoted as losing patience with men who had become too accommodating and passive. "I want a man I can push up against," one woman wrote. It seems fair to say that a lot of people today are longing for a Jesus they can push up against.

That unnerves some people, including a number of our cultural gatekeepers. That *The Passion* has violated something akin to a tacit social contract established during the Enlightenment can be seen in a reflective essay by *New York Times* film critic A. O. Scott. He not only argues that the film ignores "pluralism and interreligious politesse" but also says that it dangerously blurs the lines between "sacred and secular." It seems that some of the film's most fervent admirers regard the film not as a work of art but something like the Authorized Version, a videotape of biblical history. Scott also notes, with evident distaste, that some of those involved in making the film had a number of intense spiritual experiences during the production process.

If Scott's argument were merely that some people are naïve and partisan enough to forget that *The Passion* is work of art, a human artifact, then one could hardly object (although his condescension remains revolting). But Scott goes further, I think, suggesting that it is a sinister development for our society when religious believers develop a devotional attitude toward a work of art. Here I think he is forgetting his history. Until the modern era, very few works of art in the history of man that dealt with religious texts and symbols could be cleanly divided into sacred and secular, aesthetic and liturgical. *The Divine Comedy* is a secular poem, but the hymn to the Virgin in the *Paradiso* can and has been said as a prayer. The same dynamic relationship between the aesthetic and liturgical can be said of many of the classic paintings that Gibson drew on for *The Passion,* from Caravaggio's *Deposition* to the heart-wrenchingly beautiful *Avignon Pietà,* the penultimate image of *The Passion.* In the modern era the same positive tension can be found in paintings by Georges Rouault or poems by Eliot, Auden, or Levertov.

Admittedly, the borderland between art and liturgy is rarely an inspiring place: it's more likely to be populated by kitsch than by works of tragic grandeur. But *The Passion* inhabits that sphere with some distinction; it *is* devotional in nature, an extended cinematic version of the stations of the cross.

A. O. Scott feels that *The Passion* changes the cultural rules in a way he finds threatening. In that sense, the film is what the postmodernists might call "transgressive." Of course, that's high praise when intellectuals use the word to denote works that challenge certain traditional values and institutions. But there are times when the word "politesse" is just a euphemism for a particular brand of censorship: in this case, the insistence that the public square be stripped of unsightly expressions of faith.

Roger Ebert called *The Passion* a "personal message film," and there's some truth to that, but not in the sense that one would use that phrase of, say, Oliver Stone. However individual and controversial and subject to criticism his rendition may be, Mel Gibson's message is nourished and shaped by his respect for an ancient tradition. And at the heart of that tradition is the belief in the unimaginable depth of God's passion for us.

Why the Inklings Aren't Enough

TOWARD THE END OF his life, Karl Marx found himself in conversation with an earnest would-be acolyte who was burbling about his plan to found a Marxist club. The older man suddenly rounded on him, declaring: *Je ne suis pas une Marxiste!* (I am not a Marxist). In a few simple words Marx managed not only to reject the status of cult hero but also to insinuate that systematizing his thought would falsify it.

In a similar vein, it has often been noted that the two Oxford dons at the center of the famous literary group known as the Inklings—C. S. Lewis and J. R. R. Tolkien—would be appalled by the virtual canonization that has been conferred on them by adoring fans.

What concerns me, however, is not so much the tendency of many Christians to treat these two writers as saints, as dubious as that may be. Rather, I find worrisome the fact that for many believers today, the Inklings seem to provide the sole literary diet. As we near the half-century mark since their deaths, this clinging to Lewis and Tolkien seems less a matter of homage and more an act of quiet desperation.

The problem is not the Inklings, but Inklingism.

Unfortunately, debates about the legacy of Lewis and Tolkien tend to get bogged down in wrangles between elitists and populists. The elitists argue that both writers opted for fantasy as a medium because they suffered from a form of arrested development: they created escapist realms that provided refuge from the emotional and psychological complexities of life. Populist defenders retort that the elitists are only concerned with the deviant and dysfunctional, failing to perceive the way Lewis and Tolkien celebrate virtue, goodness, and common sense.

One way to begin disentangling the half-truths underlying this debate is to place the work in context. Critic Alan Jacobs has pointed out a number of reasons for the popularity of the Inklings among American Christians:

that they were British, Oxford dons, upheld a middle-class code of common sense, were not professional theologians, and excelled as storytellers.

These are good points, but the issues run deeper. Lewis and Tolkien, along with Charles Williams and earlier British Christian writers such as Gerard Manley Hopkins, George MacDonald, and G. K. Chesterton, sought to baptize the Romantic movement. They shared with the Romantics an aversion to modern, technological society and stressed the healing powers of nature, organic form, and the dignity of the common man. With the Romantics they celebrated the Middle Ages as a time of unity and balance. Narnia and Middle Earth are essentially medieval cultures.

Many of these authors turned to the idyllic mode—in fantasy, allegory, and science fiction—to provide oases of meaning in a time of fragmentation. The Inklings championed "mythopoeic" literature, the crafting of alternate worlds where symbols and stories could heal the wounds of modern, alienated man.

At its best, this Christianized Romanticism achieved what it set out to do: to re-enchant the world. In an era of cynicism and disillusionment, the Inklings brought to life the mythic density of a sacramental vision, the sense of the sacred, even of holiness, amid the ordinariness of everyday life.

Of course, the typical attack on the Inklings takes them to task for running away from the harsh realities of mature life into the childish world of fantasy. Here the nastier comments about Lewis's sexual life are brought in, along with the fate of Susan in the *Chronicles of Narnia*, who fails to enter heaven because she prefers "nylons and lipstick and invitations" to God.

In a chapter on realism in *An Experiment in Criticism*, Lewis calls this the argument against "infantilism," and goes on to make the case for the virtues of childlike wonder, citing Tolkien as an authority. Ostensibly, Lewis is merely arguing that fantasy be given a place in the canon. Indeed, his book is a plea for tolerance and the development of a catholic taste in literature.

But here things get muddled. In this chapter and elsewhere Lewis is guilty of putting his finger on the scales: while granting that there is a distinguished tradition of realism—*Middlemarch* and *War and Peace* are his paradigms—he evinces no enthusiasm for it. He makes realism an entirely modern phenomenon, which is nearly impossible to maintain. While the realistic novel may be a recent development, realism itself is deeply woven into our culture, from the Greeks onward. It is no secret that he found little of interest in modern literature, loathing even the poetry of T. S. Eliot, a fellow defender of the faith.

The seed of Lewis's defensiveness on this point tends to blossom into the full populist fury of his defenders. But just as it is wrong to condemn the Romantic imagination, it is also wrongheaded to erect it into a self-sufficient system, which causes its own set of confusions. For example, many lovers of the Inklings don't quite know what to make of Philip Pullman, whose trilogy *His Dark Materials* employs mythopoeia to create a Nietzschean "anti-Narnia," as one writer has put it.

One does not have to deny the glories of Narnia when deploring the fate of Susan, who leaves the scene the moment she becomes sexualized— in short, the moment when she leaves childhood for the ambiguities of adulthood. In a sense, she leaves the realm of fantasy and enters the world of realism. Religious readers ought to follow her there, where her tale is told by other writers. There may be no accounting for taste, but as every nutritionist will tell you, health is dependent on a balanced diet. Those who fail to heed that advice are truly guilty of infantilism.

ART AND FAITH IN THE
PUBLIC SQUARE

The Culture Wars Revisited

TEN YEARS AGO IN these pages I attempted to explain "Why I Am a Conscientious Objector in the Culture Wars." At that time, the dust had only recently settled on the public controversies over National Endowment for the Arts funding of works by Robert Mapplethorpe and Andres Serrano. In addition to the debate over public funding of the arts, the central culture war issues had emerged: abortion, euthanasia, welfare, homosexual rights, and church/state relations. James Davison Hunter had followed up his groundbreaking book *Culture Wars* with the even more ominously titled *Before the Shooting Starts*.

It was clear then that we were entering a new era in American political life when "genuine debate and reflection on the issues [had] been replaced by the clash of factions fighting for absolutist, ideologically pure visions." What disturbed me was not merely the erosion of civility but the rapid politicization of nearly every corner of civic life. I argued:

> The urgent need at the moment is to recognize that we cannot reduce culture and its various modes of discourse to nothing more than a political battleground. The political institutions of a society grow up out of a rich cultural life, and not the other way around. As its etymology indicates, the word culture is a metaphor for organic growth. Reducing culture to politics is like constantly spraying insecticide and never watering or fertilizing the soil.

The twin sources of culture, I concluded, are art and religious faith. From these two springs come the fundamental symbols and emotional attachments of a social order. Because ideological politics tends to reduce these symbols to slogans and channel emotions into tribalistic anger and resentment, we must engage in a vigorous effort to renew our cultural life by purifying the sources.

A decade later, I stand by those words. The culture wars have gone from bad to worse. They have shifted from the grand tableaux of political

theater to the constant clamor of talking heads on cable television. They
rage in best-selling hardcover books filled with barbaric yawps. They fester
in film documentaries that have long since abandoned the canons of journalistic and historical objectivity for sneering propaganda. In addition to
Left and Right we now have Blue and Red.

In a recent *Los Angeles Times* editorial, the media critic Tim Rutten
pointed out that the ancient idea of political rhetoric as an act of persuasion, in which both parties remain open to altered perceptions and compromise, has given way to each side preaching to their respective choirs. He
likens the utopian absolutism of the culture warriors to religious fanaticism
where ranting best sellers are the equivalent of "secular apologetics." Rutten
asks: "Just how far do we want to go toward a faith-based politics?"

It's not difficult to sympathize with the question, but Rutten's language
manifests one of the deeper confusions that surround the culture wars.
Take the notion of apologetics, which refers to the systematic, rational exposition and defense of religious doctrines. In the hands of a great thinker
like Athanasius or Augustine, apologetics is an extension of theology, because great thinkers know how to balance logical extrapolation with a vivid
awareness of mystery. But in less skilled hands apologetics runs dangerously close to rationalistic shorthand. Just as politics works with the stuff of
culture, so apologetics works with the stuff of faith. To mistake something
that is secondary for the primary—the map for the experience of the journey—is to lose the spirit in the letter. So it should be no surprise that in the
era of the culture wars, apologetics has come to dominate large sectors of
the Christian discourse.

Rutten's intuition about apologetics runs aground when he uses the
word *faith* pejoratively. Faith is openness to divine mystery, an openness
that requires humility and a vivid awareness of the fragility and contingency
of our human formulations. What critics like Rutten glibly characterize as
faith is really ideology. When I was in college I studied the works of several
great political philosophers who used the term *ideology* to explain the abstract systems of ideas that formed the underpinnings of communism and
fascism. In the words of the Austrian novelist Robert Musil, an ideology is
a "second reality" imposed upon the world.

Several of the scholars I studied used the analogy of the ancient heresy of Gnosticism to illuminate their discussion of ideology. The Gnostics
believed that our world was fundamentally evil, created by an evil god.
The good god was utterly outside this world; only the gnostic elect had the

divine spark—the knowledge (*gnosis*)—that enabled them to strike through the mask of evil and attain salvation in the realm beyond the world.

It's taken me the better part of two decades since I graduated from college to realize that gnostic ideology is not confined to totalitarian regimes across the oceans but is an ever-present temptation. Once I imagined myself a foot soldier fighting in a just war. What could be more urgent, fulfilling, noble? But eventually it dawned on me that a soldier waging war for utopia can never win.

Here's something else I've concluded: the assumption that the culture wars are between Blue "progressivists" and Red "orthodox" (Hunter's terms) doesn't do justice to the complexity of the cultural and political landscape. It obscures rather than reveals. Many of those who oppose abortion are wedded to a political philosophy that embraces a strain of liberalism (running through Adam Smith to John Stuart Mill and beyond) that celebrates individual rights and the glories of "freedom of choice." Espousing a tradition that extols freedom and individualism above virtue and community ultimately makes for the sort of consumerist society in which abortion is an inevitable "right." Perplexities like this abound.

Once upon a time, the culture wars were exclusively about domestic, social issues, but in our brave new world they extend to foreign policy. America is either the world's salvation or the cause of all its problems. What of those who support America's justification for occasionally taking action beyond our borders without global consensus but who believe we are now doing so with a foolish lack of historical or cultural sensitivity? They will be stoned by Reds and Blues alike.

As more than one wag has said, there are two types of people in this world: those who divide the world up into two kinds of people and those who don't.

My editorial of ten years ago, along with texts by half a dozen other writers, was the subject of extensive criticism by Reformed scholar John Bolt in his book *A Free Church, a Holy Nation.* Those who had publicly dissented from the culture wars were espousing, he wrote, "cultural pacifism" that played directly into the hands of the enemy. Despite his affection for words like "cobelligerency" and "jihad" (his book was published just before 9/11), Professor Bolt is a serious thinker as well as a culture warrior. To the extent that he believes the culture wars have an ultimate, apocalyptic significance, I disagree with him. On the other hand, if he is arguing that no one can set themselves above politics, I am with him. Being an intelligent participant in political life is a responsibility everyone should embrace.

But in his passion for total war, Professor Bolt doesn't seem to believe that there should be any civilians tending to other matters back home: everyone should be armed and dangerous. The brilliant poet, philosopher, and political thinker Charles Péguy, who wrote in the heat of France's culture wars of the early twentieth century, understood the all-consuming demands of modern ideological politics. Péguy's analysis carries weight precisely because he was an utterly political animal. But he also understood the role of culture in maintaining a healthy polity. So he could write with some authority about political activists who scorn those who look after a society's *mystique,* the religious and imaginative symbols and narratives that give a culture its identity:

> For the politically minded always recover their balance, and think they can save themselves, by saying that they at least are practical, and that we are not. That is precisely where they are mistaken. Where they mislead. We do not even grant them that. It is the mystic who is practical, and the politically minded who are not. It is we who are practical, *who do something,* and it is they who are not, *who do nothing.* It is we who accumulate and they who squander. It is we who build, lay foundations, and it is they who demolish. It is we who nourish, and they who are the parasites.

A socialist turned Catholic, Péguy became convinced that in the modern era "Everything begins as a *mystique* and ends as a *politique.* . . . [T]he mystique should not be devoured by the politique to which it gave birth." As Alexander Dru writes in the introduction of *Temporal and Eternal,* the book from which these quotes are taken, Péguy believed in the need for "Christianity always to return to its source, its *mystique,* and to *refound* its institutions by allowing the *mystique* the freedom to create tradition afresh."

Here's the irony: the one force at the heart of the West's *mystique* that has the resources to serve as a source of social and cultural renewal—the Judeo-Christian tradition—has become to millions of people a sign of division and ideological fanaticism. The blame for this lies not simply at the hands of that tradition's avowed enemies, but among the faithful, too. Péguy reserved his greatest fury for the Catholic clergy, whom he felt had given in to politicization and forgotten to tend to the *mystique.*

The choice is not between engaging in political life and nurturing culture. Both are essential activities. But given the huge disproportion between the energies and resources being devoted to these endeavors, the real question is how many of those addicted to the culture wars will be willing to step back, refound institutions, and create tradition afresh.

There are signs that a movement in this direction has already begun. The efforts are small—insignificant, even, at least to some eyes. But then a number of world-changing movements have begun in just that way. A group called Brewing Culture meets at a pub in the shadow of the nation's capitol for the purpose of "creating, commissioning, and celebrating transcendent works of art and media." On the web publication called the New Pantagruel, a growing number of young, renegade conservatives buck the dominant trends on the Right with Rabelaisian wit and gusto. Another online magazine, Godspy, moves Catholic discourse away from mere apologetics into probing reflections, including moving personal narratives grounded in experience.

As huge armies march past, these small groups accumulate, build, nourish. Together, they form what Péguy called a "system of courage."

Always Now

ARE YOU CONVINCED THAT everything is going to hell in a handbasket? Down the tubes? Or are you possessed of a more sanguine temperament? Do you feel that life is getting better every day in every way? Do you believe in progress or regress? What would the make and model of your handbasket happen to be?

The older I get, the more interested I am in people's convictions about the *directionality* of history.

I have been told that there were times when the doctrine of progress was in the ascendant, when millions of people believed that society was moving inexorably toward utopia. But every time I investigate such a period, I find the evidence contradictory at best. For example, some people point to the time after World War I when the Russian Revolution and the League of Nations were held up as beacons of hope. But in that time I also note the rise of existentialist despair, surrealism, and the popularity of Spengler's *The Decline of the West*.

Or take the 1950s, when the glossy magazines were filled with pictures of gleaming model cities—Cities of the Future!—and immaculate suburbs. At the movies film noir was painting a different, grittier sort of canvas, replete with beauty that was too good to be true, disguising the deep insecurities of a generation still reeling from a world war and the Holocaust.

Some people believe in Up, some in Down, but my guess is that most people skew toward Down. Perhaps this should be taken as little more than a form of moral common sense, a recognition of the human tendencies toward greed, lust, and the hunger for power to become solvents that break down the rights and protections we put up as bulwarks against self-interest. Since it is easier to erode such bulwarks than to build them up, our sense of decline is, in part, a form of moral realism.

Still, I can't help but feel that we suffer today from an excess of what I've come to call *declinism*, a pathological belief that things were once much better and are now skittering toward the apocalypse.

Two forces lend legitimacy to declinism: the power of technology and the rise of virulent political ideologies. Both forces not only seem to be speeding up the pace of change but also to be meddling with the building blocks of being itself: the atom, DNA, the biosphere, the family, the integrity and coherence of the nation-state. Each of these things contributes to our sense of identity, and tampering with identity is always the most disturbing of sensations.

To lose one's identity is to believe that something vital—literally life-giving—is coming to an end. In her book *For the Time Being* Annie Dillard puts it this way:

> Is it not late? A late time to be living? Are not our heightened times the important ones? For we have nuclear bombs. Are we not especially significant because our century is?—our century and its unique Holocaust, its refugee populations, its serial totalitarian exterminations, our century and its antibiotics, silicon chips, men on the moon, and spliced genes?

Dillard's words were published in 2000. That they already seem slightly dated may be the first clue that something is amiss in the declinist way of thinking. A European living through the Thirty Years' War might well have felt that the musket, religious conflict, and the rise of the "divine right of kings" and other forms of political absolutism signified the end of history.

But history went rolling right along.

Another hint that declinism is itself a problem is that it so easily transcends party lines. Is there much difference between the conservative who believes that freedom and enterprise and family values are being slowly but inevitably eroded and the liberal who believes that freedom and the environment and civil rights are on their last legs? To argue with either is to risk being told that the alternative to apocalypse is apathy.

Here I will confess that this is one of the many arguments I have with myself. Raised as a conservative, I once envisioned myself as the scourge of a decadent world; I would be the tragic hero working tirelessly to stem the onrushing tide of communism abroad and socialism at home. It made me feel important.

Then communism and socialism were more or less soundly thrashed on the world stage, with a few eccentric exceptions. Yet this historic turning of tides had little effect on my conservative friends, who managed to be just as obsessed with decline as ever.

Even now I love the prophetic voice—the religious or artistic figure who can open our eyes to injustice, narcissism, and pride. And I remain a fan of satire, that stinging form of humor employing irony and absurdity to hold up a mirror to our culture's follies and vanities—to the forms of decline that richly deserve castigation.

But in my late twenties I realized that I would never be a prophet or a satirist. Nor could I sustain a life on the basis of unrelenting criticism and negativity.

Though I've always been a pretty sturdy fellow—more workhorse than thoroughbred—I think it's fair to say that I went through something of a breakdown at that point. Out of that crisis came a change of heart. To be sure, I could chart many dark declivities in recent times, but I had begun to notice some modest but significant breakthroughs, recoveries, and revivals, too. For one thing, it became clear that a growing number of artists and writers were braving their fear of criticism by secular critics to create art that bore witness to the experience of faith, renewing an ancient tradition.

I also felt an urge I hardly understood, but which seemed to amount to this: the need to build, rather than tear down. Suddenly it became more important for me to search out and celebrate the good than to denigrate the bad, to promote the original creative voice rather than the negative and polemical.

I am not in favor of apathy, nor do I believe that people should not condemn what is wrong. There are many vocations in the world of culture and ideas, and I am not narrow enough to believe my choice is the only valid one. But I do worry that declinism is so pervasive, that it has given rise to so much anger and frustration and shrillness that it now stands in the way of reform and renewal. In the end, declinism contributes to social gridlock.

One could write whole libraries about the role that religion plays in the business of Up or Down. The millenarian impulse—the desire to use coercion to institute a realm of perfect purity, a return to some lost Eden—while it is hardly exclusive to religion, has certainly been taken up by it often enough.

But faith ought to make us feel *less* oppressed by decline, rather than more. The preoccupation with rise or fall now appears to me a projection of the perennial human temptation to live in the past or the future rather than the present. We live burdened by what we have lost or preoccupied with something we don't have but need in order to be happy.

Faith, according to the Letter to the Hebrews, is "the substance of things hoped for." That phrasing, from the King James Version, hasn't been improved upon in recent translations. In faith, what is hoped for becomes present, substantial. To live in faith means to live in the present, to know that the substance of grace is here and now. That is not to say that faith involves some sort of simple possession; it is, rather, to exist in the tension between the presence we encounter and the sense of what that presence means for our destiny. As the critic George Steiner put it in *Real Presences,* we live on Holy Saturday, between the death and loss of Good Friday and the promise of resurrection on Easter Sunday.

Annie Dillard, a wise woman, has an answer for the questions she poses about ours being a late time, a uniquely important one. It is, quite simply, no. "These times of ours are ordinary times, a slice of life like any other."

> There were no formerly heroic times, and there was no formerly pure generation. There is no one here but us chickens, and so it has always been: a people busy and powerful, knowledgeable, ambivalent, important, fearful, and self-aware; a people who scheme, promote, deceive, and conquer; who pray for their loved ones, and long to flee misery and skip death. It is a weakening and discoloring idea, that rustic people knew God personally once upon a time—or even knew selflessness or courage or literature—but that it is too late for us. In fact, the absolute is available to everyone in every age. There never was a more holy age than ours, and never a less. There is no less holiness at this time—as you are reading this—than there was the day the Red Sea parted. . . . In any instant the sacred may wipe you with its finger. In any instant the bush may flare, your feet may rise, or you may see a bunch of souls in a tree. In any instant you may avail yourself of the power to love your enemies; to accept failure, slander, or the grief of loss; or to endure torture. Purity's time is always now.

Marx called religion the opiate of the masses while offering the drug of happiness in some future revolution. Faith, far from making us apathetic, enables us to be present to what surrounds us. It also provides a sense of peace, which is always a better platform for action than anger or grievance. Saint Francis didn't stand on a soapbox in Assisi hectoring the rich about the plight of the poor; he asked those who had bread to give him some and then he delivered it to those who didn't. And you can be sure that as he did so, he didn't feel important at all.

Two-Way Traffic

IN A RECENT ESSAY, poet Ira Sadoff issued a sweeping denunciation of what he calls the "spiritualization of American poetry." Entitled "Trafficking in the Radiant" and published in the *American Poetry Review,* the essay asserts that contemporary poets have been influenced by the resurgence of religiosity in our culture, with disastrous results. "My contention is that using religion as a metaphorical expression of our powerlessness . . . diminishes human agency and makes possible a hierarchical authoritarianism . . . [and] that the Romantic desire to transcend materiality leads to a flight from the social and the sexual."

In short, Sadoff holds that the tendency of religion to "privatism and escape" generates a passivity in the face of unjust and oppressive political and social structures. Because "virtually all conventional Christian theologies" elevate the spirit above the body and the individual over the community, they make us "long to tame the dangers of living in this world."

As evidence he points to the replacement of Neruda and Larkin as poet-icons by Rilke and a newly rehabilitated T. S. Eliot. His survey of the poetry he criticizes consists of five lines by Richard Wilbur and seventeen from a poem by W. S. Di Piero. Sadoff then lists about a dozen poets as traffickers in the "radiant impalpable." The bulk of the essay is then given over to a discussion of a painting by Veronese and Eliot's anti-Semitism.

Now I confess that it would be easy to dismiss Sadoff's piece as a minor salvo in a rather remote corner of the culture wars. One might defend such a dismissal by pointing out the errors of fact and interpretation that plague the essay, beginning with misspellings, including Eliot's poem "Gerontion" (given as "Gerontin").

Even more aggravating is Sadoff's guilt-by-association name-dropping, where individual poets are tarred with an obscenely broad brush. Toss in his accusations of nostalgia for dated writers and thinkers such as the New Critics while quoting liberally from the even hoarier Freud, Sartre, and (indirectly) Marx. Finally, add a number of disingenuous statements—that he doesn't want to "re-hash" Eliot's anti-Semitism (after doing so for several paragraphs), that there is a "wide spectrum of Christian beliefs" though a few inches further down "virtually all" such beliefs are odious—and the temptation to dismiss the case becomes strong indeed.

But beyond these distractions Sadoff's central thesis deserves to be engaged. It's one of the oldest charges leveled against biblical religion, and as soon as it is made it becomes bogged down in contradictions. In one breath it is said that religion makes people passive, and in the next breath the same individuals are castigated for their activism in the public sphere. In fact, faith has always fostered social action.

For example, the political causes of the decade from 1965 to 1975, which Sadoff celebrates, are impossible to understand without reference to the religious forces at work in the civil rights and anti-war movements, including not only such public figures as Martin Luther King Jr., Dorothy Day, and Abraham Joshua Heschel, but prominent poets like Thomas Merton and Denise Levertov.

The problem with religion is that what seems on the outside to be contradiction is, from the inside, felt as the mysterious truth of paradox. To be in the world but not of it may appear to some as escapism, but those who have followed those words truly have loved the creation with a ferocious tenderness. Just look at the life curling around and bursting from the margins of ancient, illuminated prayer books—or at the children hidden in Eliot's rose garden.

The privileged role of literature is that it can serve as a bridge between the public and the private. You do not have to believe what Dante or Donne or Hopkins believed to understand something about how that faith is enacted in language. As I said in another editorial, these works become "secular Scriptures."

The negative phenomena Sadoff condemns are hardly the exclusive possession of religious people. They are perennial human problems. The fear of powerlessness and the urge to cram truth and mystery into narrow, rigid propositions have led not only to authoritarian religious structures but also to atheistic, totalitarian regimes. Like most culture warriors, Sadoff uses his mighty sword to cleave the world in exactly the wrong direction.

Here's the twist: in contemporary poetry, some of the most subtle explorers of the goodness of the body, the contingency of human knowledge, and the need for a politically engaged community are those poets who are revisiting, often with fear and trembling, the biblical tradition.

Far from privileging the spirit over the body, Richard Wilbur's most famous poem is "Love Calls Us to the Things of This World." Denise Levertov's embrace of the Catholic Church did nothing to dampen her social conscience or mute her prophetic voice. Scott Cairns entitled one of his collections *Recovered Body*, precisely because he shares Sadoff's concern with the gnostic tendencies of many believers. Moreover, Cairns's constant theme is confluence between the mystical Christianity of the East and postmodern ideas about the elusiveness of presence.

Sadoff ends his essay with the assertion that "*because* our lives are finite, every choice matters." You can derive that thought from existentialism . . . or from the book of Genesis. The world is a dangerous place, and one of its dangers is the human will. American poetry will be best served if poets and critics alike, religious or not, limn the possibilities—and limits—of human agency.

Keeping a Private Address

REVIEWING A RECENT BIOGRAPHY of the writer Eudora Welty, Francine Prose confessed that before reading the book she had imagined the author as "a bit like Emily Dickinson with excellent southern manners, or perhaps a more robust, less God-haunted Flannery O'Connor—one of those stay-at-home prodigies who somehow acquire an intimate knowledge of human experience without venturing far beyond the garden gate." Despite the biographies detailing her wide travels and far-flung friendships, despite the volumes of her photographs, which demonstrate her eye for the public world, the myth of Welty as recluse has been slow to die.

Though a much beloved, even lionized figure, Miss Welty has had her critics, particularly among those who patrol the quotient of political engagement—or perceived lack of engagement—on the part of various writers and artists. Indeed, Welty wrote a famous essay entitled "Must the Novelist Crusade?" that answers the question in the negative. In that essay she wrote:

> Writing fiction is an interior affair. Novels and stories always will be put down little by little out of personal feeling and personal beliefs arrived at alone and at firsthand over a period of time as time is needed. To go outside and beat the drum is only to interrupt, interrupt, and so finally to forget and to lose. Fiction has, and must keep, a private address. For life is lived in a private place; where it means anything is inside the mind and heart.

This has been taken to signal Welty's belief that the artist should retreat from the public sphere and thus avoid the moral imperative of addressing social injustice.

Setting aside for a moment whether this is a fair characterization of her argument, one thing is sure: as one scans the cultural landscape more than forty years after Miss Welty's essay was published, it is clear that the landscape is replete with artist-crusaders—or, as they are even more inelegantly called these days, artist-activists. And amid the self-righteous posturing, much is being lost.

To say this is not to advocate a retreat into the palace of art, or to deny that artists are citizens with an obligation to speak the truth as they see it and to participate in the political process. There is nothing wrong with writing a poem and then publishing an op-ed in a newspaper or magazine, or even appearing at a rally for a candidate or cause. It might be possible to discuss the issue of proportionality, but that is merely a prudential issue, not a matter of principle.

What concerns me is the growing trend that leads writers and artists to feel impelled to make their ideological commitments the defining characteristic of their creative work. It is a commonplace that our cultural elite are secular and cavalier about morality, but the problem with the world today is not too little morality, but too much. The pathology of moralism is often laid at the feet of religion—and God knows that there's plenty of history to fuel that assertion—but many of the most earnest Puritans today are self-described secularists.

Compared to the crude morality tales of the past, the current crop of high-minded art is often more sophisticated, more circumspect about its edifying intentions. But look carefully and you can detect all the hallmarks of the Puritan sensibility: the tendency to reduce drama and ambiguity to allegory, where characters devolve into types and abstractions; the use of particular issues as illustrations (domestic violence, say, instead of drunkenness or lechery); the movement toward a concluding moral or a purgation of the malefactors.

The old compact between the artist and the recipient of the art—that one interacts with the work as if on a journey of exploration—has been abrogated. If you open a novel by a writer like Barbara Kingsolver, who established and funded the Bellwether Prize for the Literature of Social Change, are you a reactionary for questioning the social import of her story? When Anne Lamott peppered her latest book, *Plan B,* with a series of snarly asides criticizing President George W. Bush, even many of her fans felt left out in the cold. Significantly, her earlier book, *Traveling Mercies,* which left little doubt about its author's basic political outlook, continues to outsell *Plan B* by a large margin.

It would be wrong to see the politicization of art as the pet project of the avant-garde; it's a thoroughly mainstream phenomenon. In fact, it's big business. The reigning queen of moral self-improvement in America,

Oprah Winfrey, has turned it into a book club. While I'm as grateful as any writer to Winfrey for still caring about the written word, and for occasionally including classic authors such as William Faulkner on her list, more often than not she selects books that are little more than thinly veiled advertisements for the therapeutic mentality. Which might be defined as the care and nurture of one's personal sense of well-being. One might even assign the titles of Oprah episodes to some of these novels: *Coping with Grief. Escaping a Bad Relationship. Aging Gracefully: The Best is Yet to Come!*

In short, the new literature of righteous feeling prefers melodrama to either comedy or tragedy.

One of the classic forms of artistic engagement with the public realm has been the comic form known as satire, but satire is in a bad way, too. The best satire available today is on television—whether on Comedy Central or *The Simpsons*. Since television is a self-referential medium that lends itself to self-parody, one can see why satire flourishes there. There was a time during the early days of New Journalism when satire seemed to be making a comeback, particularly in the early essays and articles of Tom Wolfe. But ever since Wolfe decided that he was the reincarnation of Charles Dickens, his long, bloated novels only demonstrate satiric energy in brief flashes.

The dearth of satire in high literature and art is an outright loss. The great satirists, such as Aristophanes, Juvenal, Erasmus, Swift, Hogarth, and Waugh, combined a relish for anarchic mayhem with a strong moral sensibility. That is the paradox of satire: the anarchic defense of order. Because the best satire works through irony, it tends to respect the intelligence of its readers—allowing space for the gaps to be filled and the topsy-turvydom to be made right, if only in one's mind. Another virtue of satire is its ability to demonstrate how private vices and foibles become magnified and transformed into public disorder and hypocrisy.

Nor is tragedy compatible with the sort of boosterism that attends the art of "social change." This is undoubtedly because tragedy calls the very notion of progress into question, revealing the contingent nature of our experience and what Samuel Johnson called "the vanity of human wishes." And yet tragedy is one of the highest forms of artistic engagement with political life. One of the traditional modes of tragedy involves the terrifying conflict between two good things. For Antigone, it is the private, sacred imperative to honor the dead against the good of obedience to lawful authority.

One of the few writers capable of this sort of tragic vision today is Cormac McCarthy, particularly in his Border Trilogy. McCarthy is one of those figures likely to be deemed insufficiently political, but among the many achievements of this trilogy is that it holds up a mirror to American efforts to bring about justice in the world. The two protagonists, John Grady Cole and Billy Parham, are virtuous American heroes: self-reliant, compassionate, rooted in the ancient rhythms of nature. Yet whenever they cross the border to another culture in order to bring about justice, they bring ruin on themselves and those they love. In their attempts to restore something lost or to retrieve something stolen, they fail to see that their efforts to do good cause grief and suffering, without obtaining their object. There are times when suffering and endurance are better than action, even when action is undertaken for virtuous reasons. A dark vision, perhaps, but one that can elicit more profound reflection on the pros and cons of American intervention around the world than an entire library of contemporary politicized books.

Though there are many pitfalls awaiting the would-be artist-activist, I believe it is possible to pursue this course with both dignity and respect for the integrity of art. The model I would uphold is Wendell Berry, who is both an extraordinarily gracious man and a man of adamantine—some would say extreme—principles. Berry has long been a champion of environmental causes and a harsh critic of big business. His ideas may provoke strong reactions, but his words are temperate, measured. What gives his writing about political matters such resonance and gravitas is that it emerges out of geography, history, and community. His opinions are less constructed than they grow organically from his life. And because his community is rooted in a particular soil, his advocacy avoids feeling narrow and ideological.

Berry's poetry and fiction are rooted in private experience—love, marriage, family, work—and yet the Kentucky farmers he writes about are public-spirited people. After all, the public realm begins with one's neighbors, and his characters spend a great deal of time in each other's company. No one in a Berry novel could say, with a Dostoyevsky character, that they love mankind but can't stand their neighbors.

There is a saying that all politics is local, but perhaps another truth is that we all bring our private lives into the public realm. To say that art has a private address, as Eudora Welty did, is not to refuse a moral imperative; it is to remind us that both art and life begin in the immediacy and concreteness of the local. A whole book of essays has been published demonstrating how Miss Welty's stories contain "responses to public political issues—political corruption, racial apartheid, poverty, McCarthyism, and the Rosenberg trials, violent resistance to the civil rights movement, and southern reverence for identities of the cultural past." But our response to the great issues of the day begins with the way we cook meals, greet one another, do our jobs, and raise our families.

According to Welty, "great fiction shows us not how to conduct our behavior but how to feel. Eventually, it may show us how to face our feelings and face our actions and to have new inklings about what they mean."

It may sound like heresy, but I believe that religion is as much about how to feel as it is how to behave. In the end, the best antidote to moralism run amok is true religion, not secularism. About a year before his election to the papacy, Joseph Ratzinger gave the funeral homily for an Italian priest named Luigi Giussani, who had founded a lay movement that had nearly disintegrated in the political turmoil of the late 1960s. Ratzinger characterized Giussani's vision—a vision that successfully moved beyond that upheaval—in this way: "Christianity is not an intellectual system, a packet of dogmas, a moralism, Christianity is rather an encounter, a love story; it is an event." He went on to say:

> It was the great temptation of that moment to transform Christianity into a moralism and moralism into politics, to substitute believing with doing. Because what does faith imply? We can say, "In this moment we have to do something." And all the same, in this way, by substituting faith with moralism, believing with doing, we fall into particularisms, we lose most of all the criteria and the orientations, and in the end we don't build, we divide.

In art, as in faith, the heart of the matter is not doing, but the wonder we experience—the way we feel—in the face of the encounter. And we are never more willing to change and to build than when we fall in love.

Conservative Elegies

Bliss was it in that dawn to be alive,
But to be young was very heaven!
—William Wordsworth

Within just a few weeks of each other, America recently lost two of its finest sons—William F. Buckley Jr. and E. Victor Milione. One was known to millions, while the other preferred obscurity, but both were seminal figures in the modern revival of political and intellectual conservatism. I eulogize them together not only because of their shared convictions, but for a simple reason: they were my first two employers. They literally gave me my start in life.

In the summer of 1980, I could be pardoned for feeling like William Wordsworth at the time of the French Revolution: a new dawn was breaking and I was an idealistic youth ready to become an ardent herald for that sunrise.

I was not yet twenty-one, and yet I had a strong sense of the historic nature of the moment. My father had left a lucrative career in advertising to become a pioneering member of the conservative movement; he was sitting in the room in 1953 when the young William F. Buckley Jr. came to pitch the idea of a new magazine, to be called *National Review,* to a group of movement leaders.

By the time I graduated in May from a college known for its close association with conservatism, Ronald Reagan had wrapped up the Republican nomination for president. The hostage crisis in Iran was dragging on, and President Carter's doleful moral earnestness was faltering in the face of Reagan's buoyant wit and actor's poise.

Like the son of an exiled king, I looked forward to Revolution and Restoration.

As the heat waves shimmered off the sidewalks of Manhattan, I had a ringside seat at *National Review*—Ronald Reagan's favorite magazine—where I had won the summer internship gig. The atmosphere in the cluttered offices on East Thirty-fifth Street was electric, and never more so than at the biweekly editorial meetings, when outside contributors would come to New York and join the regular staff, and the editorials for the issue to come would be assigned.

The summer intern at *NR* might have had to sort the mail, but he or she was also allowed to submit paragraphs for the unsigned editorial section at the beginning of the magazine. That meant I got to sit in on the editorial meetings. When Bill Buckley was in town he would chair these sessions. He sat at one end of the conference table, rumpled of shirt, aquiline of nose, sporting the trademark grin that seemed to stretch his face a bit too tight. His limbs always seemed akimbo—he would prop his legs up on the table and lean over to one side, achieving configurations that would have made a circus contortionist proud.

I sat through these gatherings, transfixed and more than a little intimidated. I might have been a big man on my college campus, but in the editorial offices at *NR* I felt out of my depth. Writing those editorial paragraphs was almost more than I could handle: you had to be witty, droll, knowledgeable, *and* politically savvy, all at once. Bill once returned one of my efforts with a single word in red ink at the top: *Banal.*

Though I knew instantly that he was right, I couldn't help but feel devastated.

While he may have been a tough editor, and perhaps a little unfeeling with that comment, Bill was unfailingly kind to me in person. In the years after I left *NR*, Bill would write forewords for two of my books. When I sent him the pilot issue of *Image* he sent a check for a thousand dollars, becoming our second donor. Nothing about *Image* served any immediate agenda of his.

Anthony Dolan, in his own tribute to Buckley, noted that a young friend of his had asked him why those writing eulogies to WFB could not write "more on the great man himself and a little less on the authors and what they said, discussed, or did with the great man." Dolan's response was: "'Hard to do.' Meaning that, in writing about Bill, in appreciating him, it is just hard to leave yourself out. Or what he did for you."

Much has been said about the way he provided conservatism with an urbane, sophisticated face, and the diplomatic skills he wielded, bringing together the coalition of disparate sects and interest groups that triumphed in 1980.

All that is true, but it misses a deeper truth. Whatever you make of his political positions, Bill Buckley served the commonweal because he cared above all about language. His love of esoteric words became something of a running joke, one that he played up (as in his championing of the word *steatopygous*), and he was known to be a master logician.

But Bill was devoted to the art of rhetoric—not in the modern, pejorative sense of the word but in the ancient sense of the judicious and precise use of persuasive speech. He loved the power of ideas, but he understood their tendency to become abstractions. He ceaselessly offered homage to the thinkers he admired and never pretended to be, and he undertook to translate their concepts into contextualized speech—into real-world situations. In this sense he also upheld another ancient principle: that of prudence, the wise application of principle to ambiguous situations. He was known occasionally to change his mind and to break ranks with fellow conservatives when he felt strongly about an issue.

Despite a strong libertarian streak, Bill's vision was grounded in a rich, Catholic conception of life. He might have opposed church pronouncements that seemed to rely too heavily on government solutions to social issues, but he championed the Catholic concept of subsidiarity, the idea that problems should be solved not from above, but from the local, immediate places of neighborhood, family, and voluntary association.

Above all, he was a political commentator who knew how little politics could really change the world. Many of those who met him marveled that in private conversation he almost never spoke of politics. The topic was more likely to be Bach, or the pleasures of sailing.

In an era of ideological polarization and broadcast barbarism, Bill Buckley stood for responsible political engagement—precisely because that engagement drew its sustenance from deep cultural and philosophical roots.

When I left the employ of *National Review* I took a position at the Intercollegiate Studies Institute, an organization that sought to defend conservatism in academia.

ISI's president, E. Victor Milione, was, in most regards, the polar opposite of Bill Buckley. Bill was gregarious, extroverted—a born performer, whether in front of a typewriter, television camera, or harpsichord. Vic Milione may have been the shyest man I ever met. He often struck people as taciturn, but when he laughed, you felt that the world had just received a last-minute reprieve from the apocalypse.

Bill was famous, his life a blur of movement from transatlantic sailing trips to talk shows to the commencement circuit. Vic was known only to a few, and his greatest gift was his immovability.

Vic Milione presided over ISI for many years. He, too, had the ability to bring various factions together in a lively, if contentious, coalition. As conservatism gained political power, he was repeatedly approached by donors who promised large sums of money in exchange for ISI's becoming more heavily political. While he held strong political convictions, Vic believed that ISI should remain academic in character, devoted to scholarship rather than the promotion of platforms.

Even as conservatism swept into office in the 1980s, Vic sensed the dangers of power. One of those dangers was the suppression of thought in favor of a party line. When I made some of ISI's programs and publications a little edgier, stirring up what I thought was healthy intellectual debate, Vic stoutly defended me from those who preferred a more bland and placid approach. He probably lost some grant money in the process.

Vic stubbornly resisted the lures of power and money, preferring a leaner organization to selling out. He saw ISI's mission as the defense of the western synthesis of classical philosophy and the Judeo-Christian tradition. Vic—whose father was a sculptor and gardener—held that politics can be changed only when culture changes, and that culture is enriched not by the hardened positions and shrill pronouncements of the "culture wars" but by the matrix of imagination derived from art and faith.

Ironically, it was this vision of the world that caused me to walk away from the conservative movement. Even in the euphoria of 1980, I began to feel ambivalent about the direction of conservatism. After Reagan's election I fielded dozens of phone calls at *National Review* from right-wingers seeking references for government jobs, including some in departments that conservatives had pledged to abolish.

Later in his life, William Wordsworth came to regret his early enthusiasm for the French Revolution, preferring the conservative Edmund Burke's philosophy of slow, organic change grounded in local custom and experience to radical discontinuities brought about by fiat. It strikes me now as ironic that conservatism should so often pursue policies, whether foreign or domestic, that are redolent of the imposed abstractions of the French Revolution.

Burke believed that only the "moral imagination," which sees humanity in the light of its transcendent destiny, could oppose the forces of politicization, which strips us down to categories. Burke, too, was a man of prudence and a master of rhetoric. For Burke, the problem was not change—because life is always changing—but how to adapt ancient truths to current circumstances.

I still understand the mission of *Image*—presenting contemporary art and literature that engage the Judeo-Christian tradition—as honoring the older, humbler vision of Burkean conservatism espoused by great men like Bill Buckley and Vic Milione.

May we see their like again. *Requiescant in pace.*

Poetic Justice

The following is adapted from an address given at the Wild Goose Festival in Corvallis, Oregon, on September 1, 2012.

BEFORE I CAME DOWN here to deliver this talk on how art and social justice should—and shouldn't—mix, I posted on Facebook that I was preparing by reading the works of various writers. One commentator singled out Gustave Flaubert from my list and responded with a skeptical "Hmm." I understood the reaction: after all, Flaubert was known as a writer who cared more for style than social justice ("One never tires of what is well-written, style is life!"). In contrast to the two other great social realists of nineteenth-century French fiction—Honoré de Balzac and Émile Zola—Flaubert rarely wrote about the poor and downtrodden. His masterpiece, *Madame Bovary*, told the story of a provincial woman, the wife of a bourgeois doctor, who enters into two adulterous affairs, shops her way into bankruptcy, and ultimately kills herself. Zola's masterpiece, *Germinal*, on the other hand, is a bleak, searing depiction of the coal miners' strike in northern France in the 1860s.

Yet Flaubert is the more widely read author today. One could take this fact and surmise that readers prefer style over substance, lurid subject matter over the plight of the working poor. But I think there's something more going on. I am not so much interested in disparaging works like *Germinal*, which have social justice at the forefront of their concerns, as I am intrigued by the possibility that a work of art like *Madame Bovary* may in the end serve the cause of justice more deeply and lastingly—and thus serve as a model for those of us who care about both art and justice.

Emma Bovary's story, though set a century and a half ago, has a startlingly contemporary feel. A beautiful young woman from the country with passion and dreams marries a doctor who turns out to be a dull, plodding fellow. What first appeared to her as a gateway into a larger world has become the door clanging shut on a prison cell. The two men with whom she has affairs seem to come from worlds that offer richness, refinement, beauty—the higher forms of life for which she yearns. One is a budding intellectual and law student, the other a wealthy man who lives in a quasi-aristocratic chateau. Each offers her a path toward an enticing future. Both abandon her.

A summary this brutally brief makes it sound like she enters into these relationships casually, but that's not the case. Still, the reader does not have to condone Emma's infidelities to harbor at least some pity and sympathy for her naïveté, her restless desire to be overtaken and overwhelmed by something grand and ecstatic.

Flaubert knows that we see more than Emma does and that we will be tempted to imagine ourselves above her. If we can avoid that trap—if we can avoid committing an injustice against the protagonist—it may be possible to ask the question that should be flickering at the back of our minds: how did she get to be this way and who should be helping her?

Emma's education with the nuns, while it gives her the catechism, turns out to be more of a finishing school than a place of learning and piety, where she reads romantic novels and indulges in sentimental reveries. "Instead of following the Mass, she used to gaze at the azure-bordered religious drawings in her book. She loved the sick lamb, the Sacred Heart pierced with sharp arrows, and poor Jesus falling beneath his cross."

When Emma's affairs and shopping sprees spiral out of control, there is no one who can reach out to her. She turns to a priest but he is spiritually tone-deaf. He sees that she is in distress but when she says "it is no earthly remedy I need" all he can say is that she may have indigestion. Homais the chemist, who ought to be a trustworthy representative of the merchant class, turns out to be a cut-rate ideologue, a freethinker who fancies himself a new Voltaire, but who is oblivious to the human drama around him.

And so it goes for Emma: every sector of society that should be there for her is lost in its own pettiness and pretension. As the Southern novelist and critic Andrew Lytle once said of this novel:

> The bourgeoisie appears not as a class among classes, but as *the* class, which has usurped every estate, institution, trade, occupation, vocation, avocation in the world which victimizes Madame Bovary. Having the bourgeois mind as the only mind exposes the monstrous deformity and impossibility of such a world, a world entirely material. The isolated ego, money, physical appetites, the categories of the mortal sins (without the promise of redemption)—such do the actors in this narrative show; such is

> the substance of the composite life parodying the divine scheme,
> Substance of the very Substance.

If we are unjust to our anti4heroine, Emma Bovary, the odds are that we will miss Flaubert's devastating indictment of an entire culture—the culture we still inhabit, where everything has become a commodity and each of us is locked up inside our private world of consumption, unable to imagine, much less to foster, the common good.

Flaubert the obsessive stylist labored mightily, as he himself once put it, to find *le seul mot juste*—the one precise word. It is possible to dismiss this as mere aestheticism—the artist locked inside his palace of art fussing over the color of the curtains. But I would counter that Flaubert's concern for language was that it be, in the deepest sense of the word, just. Ezra Pound said something similar: "The poet's job is to define and yet again define till the detail of the surface is in accord with the root in justice."

And yet it would be disingenuous to suggest that art and justice will ever willingly or gracefully dance together. They want different things. Art seeks the good of the object made; justice seeks the right distribution of goods and opportunities. Art is about making; justice is about doing. Some have attempted to combine the two into a grand unified theory. Tolstoy argued that art must seek moral ends, but Oscar Wilde countered him by reminding us that "the fact of a man being a poisoner is nothing against his prose." If you're tempted to create a moral theory of art-making, just consider whether you'd want your ethics to be determined by aesthetic choices.

The philosopher Jacques Maritain, who defended these distinctions, argued that while art and ethics, like railroad tracks, can never be made to meet, they can and must coexist in the soul of the artist. There they can live in a creative tension with one another. Justice demands that art care about the world, especially the most vulnerable, that it should refrain from getting lost in its own formal concerns, its own virtuosity. Art requires that any conception of justice be grounded in the gnarled complexity of history and the inherent ambiguity of human motives and desires.

So, guided by the example set by Flaubert, allow me to offer a few thoughts about how art and social justice might take a turn or two on the dance floor.

Didacticism means the death of art. Keats said "we hate poetry that has a palpable design upon us." By all means, create a work of imagination that delves into some aspect of social justice, but keep in mind that if your creation is not also an exploration of its subject undertaken in fear and trembling, a journey that may bring about reversals and revisions, neither you nor your audience will gain much from the experience.

Do not be afraid to make your work beautiful—to polish your prose as Flaubert did—even if it must perforce depict ugliness and degradation. For one thing, your faith should give you the confidence that in brokenness, beauty can be found. But take note of Elaine Scarry's persuasive argument in her book *On Beauty and Being Just* that beauty supports justice because it makes us care about the vulnerability and fragility of what is perceived as beautiful. As Scarry notes, citing Plato (though she could as easily have quoted Augustine or Dante), beauty enables us to move from *eros,* a sensual, immediate attraction, to *agape,* the love that seeks the good of the thing beheld.

To continue with Scarry's insights, remember that the goal of your work should be to enable both your reader and yourself to become de-centered, so that you can truly identify with the other. In this way the center moves to the margin and the margin to the center. Flaubert said "Madame Bovary, c'est moi!" and he meant it: he, too, felt the pain of innocence lost, the agony of wanting something more than earthly remedies in a world that was stolidly materialistic.

Beware the temptation of moralism, which has reached epidemic proportions in our culture, both within religious communities and outside of them. Righteousness so easily becomes self-righteousness. To my way of thinking, moralism is the opposite of true religion. The antidote to moralism is presence: not "do this," but "I'm here." Flaubert wrote: "The artist must be in his work as God is in creation, invisible and all-powerful; one must sense him everywhere but never see him." This can be taken for artistic hubris, I suppose, but another way of reading it would be to think of the author's presence as being compassionate—suffering with his characters, as I think Flaubert really did.

To care about justice, an artist does not always have to focus on the largest and most distant problems; sometimes, it is best to stick with intimate and local life. One of the most powerful aspects of *Madame Bovary* is the way it demonstrates how injustice is embedded in the very fabric of the social order, coloring the way people see the world. It isn't necessary to go to a distant shore to change how people think and feel about justice around the globe. For example, one can admire a book like Dave Eggers's *What Is the What,* which gives voice to the epic, heart-bruising story of one of the Lost Boys of Sudan. But as humble as this act of literary ventriloquism may be, the novel borders on reportage rather than art. The good news is that as more artists around the planet are being seen and heard, we are becoming the beneficiaries of their own local perspectives.

Problems like poverty, disease, and homelessness are so pervasive that they seem to require large-scale solutions—and therefore many people assume that the only artistic response of value has to come through art that utilizes mass media and pop genres to get the word out on a sufficient scale. This is an understandable but misguided notion. It plays directly into the way that social justice itself has been turned into a commodity: some instant uplift, a soaring rock ballad, and a small financial donation. In the face of this we need art that resists commodification: art that is handmade, art that penetrates beneath the surface of things and demands much, rather than skimming across the sentimental surface. If the needs that justice cries out about are deep and enduring, then the art we create should be just as deep and enduring. Only that kind of art can move people to make the sort of sacrifice justice would have them make.

In *On Beauty and Being Just* Elaine Scarry writes: "what we should wish is a world where the vulnerability of the beholder is equal to or greater than the vulnerability of the person beheld." Such a world may always live just outside our reach, but as Flaubert knew, one of the gifts of art to justice is that equalizing of vulnerability. Madame Bovary, c'est moi.

CHRISTIAN HUMANISM:
THEN AND NOW

Looking for a Renaissance

MOST EDUCATED PEOPLE, IN addition to a set of favorite authors, artists, and composers, develop a fascination for one or more historic cultures: republican Rome, say, or colonial New England or the Ming dynasty. Sometimes these passions are matters of aesthetic or intellectual taste, but often they bear a relationship to the individual's ideas about what constitutes the good life and how the ideals of a past culture might nurture and strengthen one's own. Of course, the prevailing world view of a given time period may play a role in guiding what the majority find engaging. After several centuries of admiration for ancient Greece and Rome, Europeans, swayed by the Romantic movement, turned to the Middle Ages; tired of rationalism and artifice, they saw in the medieval world a model of a more organic, earthy sensibility—attuned to nature rather than the works of man.

That such celebrations of past cultures may have a political dimension is clear enough. Ancient Rome has been embraced by groups as diverse as the founders of the United States and twentieth-century fascist regimes. Perhaps one sign of our so-called postmodern condition is that no single era of the past commands the allegiance of the public.

But religion also has an influence on our embrace of the past. If the church, subject to the inevitable cultural rhythms of decadence and renewal, is "semper reformanda" (always reforming, in the words of the early Reformers), believers may turn to a past era to rediscover a primitive purity that has been lost or a richness that has leached away. Just as the Reformers themselves looked to the earliest days of the church, as recounted in the Acts of the Apostles, so many contemporary Protestants seek out the first stages of the Reformation itself for forgotten wisdom.

The Middle Ages have long been celebrated by Christians as an era of remarkable balance between earthly and spiritual things—a "thick" culture that saw man's place in a cosmic scheme of astonishing complexity and order. And in the last twenty years a growing number have turned to the

Christian East and the patristic era for a tradition that is at once ecstatically mystical and densely liturgical, a life-giving antidote to the desiccated rationalism of the West.

The attraction that so many feel for medieval or Eastern religious cultures stems precisely from their premodern character. Toward the end of the Middle Ages, the "nominalist" school of theologians brought about a radical shift in Western thought, separating the mind from reality. As the philosopher Louis Dupré notes in *Passage to Modernity*:

> Nominalist theology effectively removed God from creation. Ineffable in being and inscrutable in his designs, God withdrew from the original synthesis altogether. The divine became relegated to a supernatural sphere separate from nature, with which it retained no more than a causal, external link. This removal of transcendence fundamentally affected the conveyance of meaning. Whereas previously meaning had been established in the very act of creation by a wise God, it now fell upon the human mind to interpret a cosmos, the structure of which had ceased to be intelligible. Instead of being an integral part of the cosmos, the person became its source of meaning. Mental life separated from cosmic being: as meaning-giving "subject" the mind became the spiritual substratum of all reality.

That a group of medieval theologians ushered modernity into the world is an irony that should not go unnoticed. But for those who love the Middle Ages and the patristic East, these cultures represent an integrated sensibility prior to the onset of anthropocentric modernity and the long withdrawal of God from Western culture. That people of faith should drink deeply from these wells is hardly objectionable.

Here's the problem. Modernity happened. There can be no going back. What is needed is a new synthesis, a vision that can encompass the subjective individual with divine being.

That's why I am convinced that religious believers should delve more deeply into the era that has traditionally been the whipping boy for the critics of modernity: the Renaissance. Few topics in Western history have been so debated as the dating, character, and meaning of the Renaissance. Few periods have been as complex and unsettling—and burdened by myths.

It is not difficult to see why those who love the medieval and patristic eras consider the Renaissance the beginning of the decline of Western civilization. After all, the very separation of the individual from nature can be blamed for the rise of modern "scientism," the worship of science and technology as instruments of human domination over nature. While religious critics of the Renaissance concede that towering artistic masterpieces were created in this era, they are quick to add that in this time the arrogant notion of the artist as genius and priest of secular culture was born. There is plenty of evidence to support both of these assertions, from the artist Cellini's vaunting autobiography to Machiavelli's meditations on political power to Francis Bacon's "knowledge is power."

But the wholesale denigration of the Renaissance typical of many Christians today rests upon another irony: the uncritical acceptance of modern myths about the period. The term *Renaissance* only came into general use in the nineteenth century, and its first great expositor was Jacob Burckhardt, whose *Civilization of the Renaissance in Italy* left the "vivid impression of rampant individualism, creative energy and moral chaos, with the supernatural sanctions and Christian traditions of the Middle Ages giving way to something more like ancient pre-Christian ways of thought," according to historian Wallace K. Ferguson.

Throughout much of the twentieth century, historiographers systematically refuted Burckhardt's picture, but old myths have a way of seeping into the culture. Nonetheless, scholars such as Charles Trinkaus, Paul Oskar Kristeller, and Giuseppe Mazzotta "have thoroughly discredited the secularist interpretation of Italian humanism," writes Dupré in *Passage to Modernity*. And many others, including Marjorie O'Rourke Boyle and James McConica, have created a rich body of scholarship on the northern Christian humanists like Erasmus, More, Vives, and Reuchlin.

One of the first myths to fall was the notion that the Renaissance constituted a major break from the medieval world. Earlier humanistic "renaissances" were pointed out, such as the twelfth-century revival of Aristotle (aided by medieval Islamic scholars). The powerful influence of medieval spiritual movements such as Franciscanism and the Brethren of the Common Life (whose most famous member was Thomas à Kempis) on later Christian humanism were carefully delineated.

More importantly, it has been shown that many of the greatest Renaissance thinkers and artists were already at work trying to find a new synthesis of self and cosmos and bring healing to the modern consciousness. The conditions they faced were strikingly like our own.

The rediscovery of pagan culture involved the question of how to approach the dialogue between secular and sacred. As the Christian humanists argued for the importance of learning from pagan culture, they deepened the theology of the incarnation, attacking the sort of dualism that compartmentalizes experience and denies the unity of truth. "For Erasmus wisdom does not consist in despoiling a humiliated paganism, but in collaborating pedagogically with its highest expression," writes Boyle.

The age of exploration began the process of globalization, and while the record of Western engagement with other cultures has been checkered at best, the greatest religious order to emerge out of the Renaissance—the Jesuits—offered some of the most humane forms of intercultural exchange on record, including the mission to the Guaraní in South America, recounted in the film *The Mission*. The Jesuit missionaries to China dressed as Mandarins and learned both the language and Confucianism before breathing a word about Jesus.

The breach between the Eastern and Western churches was healed, for a brief time, at the Council of Florence. That there were political reasons influencing this is beyond doubt, but at the same time the council would not have been possible without the assiduous work of humanist theologians striving to find common ground between the two great traditions.

The rise of science presented new powers and new temptations. Shakespeare, the last great flower of the Renaissance, would tackle this subject in *The Tempest,* where a modern magus, Prospero, learns to relinquish his dominion over nature for the reconciling power of the imagination.

The emergence of the solitary self, cut off from the community and the cosmic order, led some figures of the era to vaulting ambition and pride, while others exhibited the first symptoms of what modern thinkers would call alienation. But the period gave rise to gifted artists who were among the first to dramatize and diagnose these ills. The course of Michelangelo's art, from the assurance of the David through the magnificent but wounded humanity of the Sistine Chapel to the heavy fragility of the late, unfinished pietàs, traces a tragic vision that is wedded to a Christian understanding of suffering.

At the risk of some anachronism, I think it can be argued that the struggle between hell-for-leather Reformers and reactionary Catholics during this period can be seen in the light of what have recently been dubbed the "culture wars." Eventually, these conflicts would erupt into shooting wars that would engulf Europe in an orgy of division and destruction for over a century. What gets lost in dwelling on this conflagration are the achievements of the humanists on both sides of the theological divide: the emergence of biblical criticism and philology, the first stirrings of the discipline of history, pleas for tolerance and understanding of Jews, and programs for the education of women.

Having forgotten that these achievements took place in the Renaissance, many moderns, including the religious folk, have falsely ascribed them to the secularism of the Enlightenment rather than the Christian humanist project. Chalk this up as another historical irony.

These were troubled times, to be sure. That many of the initiatives and creations of the Renaissance were failures is beyond question. The Eastern and Western churches did not unite; the Reformation further split the church. The effort to forge a synthesis between ancient tradition and modern consciousness did not take hold, and a process of secularization did, in fact, ensue. The early efforts at reaching out to other cultures with respect were followed by harsh, colonialist methods.

But most human endeavors end in failure. The goal, to quote Samuel Beckett, has always been to "fail better." Those of us who are living on the far side of the modern experiment can gain immeasurably from a study of those who sought to create the first reconciling vision.

The Renaissance cannot offer the tranquility and order that some see, rightly or wrongly, in Eastern and medieval religious cultures. But if one of the roles of history is to be a "distant mirror," then we are going to have to learn how to love trouble. We've got heaps of it ourselves.

Giotto's Ratio

The following remarks were given at Villa Agape in Florence, Italy, on the opening evening of Image's *Florence Seminar, September 14, 2008.*

IMAGE IS A JOURNAL devoted exclusively to contemporary literature and art—to the present moment—but here we are in the cradle of the Renaissance. We have not come out of mere antiquarian curiosity, but in search of parallels to our own time and the insights we can glean from them. As an organization interested in the cross-fertilization of art and faith, and the ways that these two fundamental human experiences can renew lives and communities, we believe that the Renaissance offers a model of cultural transformation that is highly relevant to the present.

Last year, the inaugural year of this program, we concentrated our attention on the classic period of the quattrocento, the emergence of the art and architecture that would later lead to the high Renaissance. The Florentine figure who stands at the summit of this period is Masaccio, and one of the high points of the seminar last year was our visit to the Brancacci Chapel, where his dramatic frescoes ground faith in a powerful, even raw, psychological realism.

This year we have opted to turn our gaze to an earlier time, a time typically considered medieval: the end of the twelfth and the beginning of the thirteenth centuries. There are several important reasons for doing so. For one thing, we kept bumping into it last year. Masaccio, we learned, was called Giotto reborn. Then there were the vital presences of the two great mendicant orders, the Franciscans and Dominicans, and their magnificent churches here in Florence, Santa Croce, and Santa Maria Novella, with all the art they commissioned and still contain.

Another crucial motive for turning to the duecento and trecento is to dispel the still pervasive myth that the Renaissance constituted a secular turning away from the pious Middle Ages. For nearly fifty years now, scholars have been systematically dismantling the thesis made popular by Burckhardt in the nineteenth century that the Renaissance was a triumph of secular individualism. These scholars now see far more continuity between the two eras than difference, including the persistence of faith.

By the same token, it is possible to observe the seeds of the Renaissance in this earlier period, hence the theme of this year's seminar: "The First Renaissance." It was a rich, tumultuous time. In the realm of philosophy, the rediscovery of Aristotle by Thomas Aquinas and others stimulated an outburst of creative thought. And then there are the three figures we will focus on this week, three figures who would transform the face of Western culture: Saint Francis of Assisi, Giotto di Bondone, and Dante Alighieri. In so many ways, the world we know would be unthinkable without them.

Quite by accident, I happened to come to a renewed appreciation of the achievement of these three individuals when I dipped into *A Secular Age,* a masterful and challenging book by Charles Taylor, winner of the 2007 Templeton Prize. Taylor's book is nothing less than a systematic critique of modern secularism from the standpoint of a rigorous philosopher. His thesis is that the greatest myth attending secularism is the notion of its inevitability. He speaks of what he calls the "straight path" model of secularization, the idea that as Western culture evolved it gradually subtracted religion and transcendence from human thought until all that was left was mere nature and natural processes.

Taylor takes issue with the argument that the newfound medieval interest in the dignity and order in nature was a first step in turning away from the supernatural—as if Thomas Aquinas were unconsciously a modern secularist who just hadn't quite come to terms with it. I admit to being relieved, though, when Taylor shifted his discussion from philosophy to art. Turning to "the new realism in painting and sculpture," he examines the issue of nature in the work of artists like Giotto.

> That the portrayal of the Virgin and Child shows real observation of contemporary models, that there is variety and individual portraiture in religious painting, that what is represented is no longer just some universal, normative feature of the person or being encountered, as in the awesome Christ Pantocrator on the cupola of the Byzantine churches, but the traits of live individuals begin to appear: all this is frequently taken as the emergence of an extra-religious motive, alongside the religious purpose.

Not so, Taylor holds. The new celebration of nature was understood as a deeper appreciation of the doctrine of the incarnation, of Christ as the perfect fusion of human and divine natures. And this was so not only in the rarefied atmosphere of philosophy and theology but on the very concrete level of devotional life and spiritual practice. Specifically, Taylor notes that the rise of the mendicant orders signaled a shift away from the monastery as the locus of faith. The Franciscans and Dominicans brought spirituality to the lay people in the newly thriving towns of the medieval era. "A devotion grows during these centuries," he notes, "to the human Christ, the suffering Christ, where before it had been the Christ of Judgment," the Pantocrator or Divine Emperor of those Byzantine churches.

This "new vision of nature, as we see in the rich Franciscan spirituality of the life of God in the animate and inanimate things which surround us . . . brought ordinary people into focus . . . ordinary people in their individuality." Taylor believes that this is nothing less than a turning point in the history of the West, a decisive step toward the primacy of the individual that underlies nearly all our current moral and political presuppositions.

He concludes: "And so it seems to be no coincidence that one of the first reflections of this focus in painting should have been Giotto's murals in the church at Assisi. This interest in the variety and detailed features of real contemporary people did not arise alongside and extrinsic to the religious point of the painting: it was intrinsic to the new spiritual stance to the world."

It is impossible to understand Giotto and Dante without reference to Saint Francis, who died several decades before they were active. It is as if the spirit of *il poverello*, "the little poor man," had to incubate in the culture before it could be birthed in the visions of painter and poet.

The saint from Assisi is famously known as a lover of nature, but this risks sentimentalizing him. We would be wise to heed G. K. Chesterton's take on this question. For Chesterton, a "lover of nature" is already at a remove from it, making it into a pretty picture. But this is to drain the presence of grace from nature, to take it out of context. Francis saw "everything as dramatic," Chesterton writes, "distinct from its setting, not all of a piece like a picture but in action like a play. A bird went by him like an arrow; something with a story and a purpose."

And here we encounter a paradox that many have forgotten, or prefer to ignore, about Francis and his times. As Chesterton puts it, Francis can revel in nature because he has seen it in the context of the nothingness out of which it was created. As a mystic, Francis had entered the darkness of the cave and had a vision of the world turned upside down, not as resting on solid ground, but as something radically dependent—literally, hanging—on its creator. Until the emptiness of that cave becomes our own inner emptying, an embrace of poverty and simplicity, our relationship to the world is askew. The practice of self-denial known as asceticism is, for Francis, not a form of masochism, but the making of space within ourselves so that we can receive the world again, fresh as on the first day of creation.

The asceticism of Francis is often treated in the fashion Charles Taylor noted: as an unfortunate remnant of an earlier age that the saint did not know how to forsake. But it is essential to his vision, as it is to that of Giotto and Dante. It was Dante who reminded us that when we find ourselves in the dark wood, lost and confused, we must go down before we can go up; we must know the darkness in ourselves and the world before we can disown it and embrace the good. The trick, Dante says, is not to be captured by the darkness but to stand inside it looking out at the light, as Francis did. Moreover, you cannot look at a single painting by Giotto, however vibrant with color and the warmth of human love, and not sense the tragedy of sin in the shadows. Without that tragic sense we could not see the poignance and sweetness in his paintings.

Knowing those shadows—that chiaroscuro—Francis, Giotto, and Dante were able to depict the human condition in three dimensions, which is precisely what enables us to see not types, but individuals. At the same time, the saint, the artist, and the poet changed our understanding of God; without detracting from his majesty, he could no longer be seen as a radically otherworldly emperor and law-giver, but had to be experienced as brother and fellow sufferer of the world's drama. Like Dante, we are pilgrims because Christ himself walked the pilgrim road to Jerusalem, where he entered the darkness on our behalf.

But what is the relevance of all this to our own time? After all, we are not inheriting an otherworldly religiosity but centuries of secularism. It is one thing to say that the great figures of this "first Renaissance" brought us a rounded, warm humanism after generations of more abstract faith, but how does that compare to our own situation?

I believe that there is a deep pertinence to be found here. In the modern era the union of nature and grace achieved in the medieval era has been put asunder, with terrible consequences. Those who embrace nature alone find it becoming opaque and ambiguous: it becomes either something to be manipulated and conquered or a force to be worshipped. When it comes to the environment, nature is pure and inviolable, but when nature stands in the way of our desires to reshape it, particularly with regard to our own bodies, nature is an obstacle we must overcome. In short, nature no longer has a purpose and a story.

But to those who attempt to cling to grace alone, which includes most of those who consider themselves religious, faith becomes abstract, a bolt of lightning from the ether, once again a matter of rules and regulations, more like a weapon to be wielded against the ungodly than a call to love.

And so many secularists and believers float away from the world, from flesh and blood. To compensate, they adopt their own versions of a frenetic moralism, a self-righteousness imposed on the world rather than a story discovered within it.

One of the most striking innovations that Giotto introduced into the history of Western painting was to change the ratio characterizing the depiction of the human body. Whereas in earlier generations the figure was elongated, with a ratio of head to body of 1:7, Giotto reduced it to 1:6, reflecting our actual proportions. In his magnificent crucifix in Santa Maria Novella, the corpus of Christ sags with a human weight never known before in Christian art. We need to regain the burden of our humanity, that unity of nature and grace. This week I hope we will find out exactly how Francis, Giotto, and Dante can help us do just that.

Follies Worldly and Divine

IN THE SUMMER OF 1509, as he lay sick in bed, Desiderius Erasmus decided to pass the time by producing a literary gift for his friend and fellow Christian humanist, Thomas More. Within a week, he completed the *Encomium Moriae*, which can be read as either the "praise of More" or the "praise of folly."

A best seller in its own time, *The Praise of Folly* is little read today. Written before the rise of the novel, it lacks the sort of picaresque narrative structure that makes a book like *Candide* accessible to contemporary readers. The *Folly* is written in an obscure form beloved in the Renaissance: an oration—we'd call it a lecture—delivered in front of an audience by the personified Folly herself.

Not exactly a scintillating format for modern sensibilities. But if you change the analogy and think of the *Folly* as an extended stand-up comedy routine—closer to a George Carlin special on cable TV than a novel—it is possible to find a way in. And there are few books with a more urgent and immediate bearing on our current circumstances than this hastily penned satire. Concealed within its comic riffs lies a vision of faith that speaks truth to an ideological age like our own.

Folly's declamation is ostensibly a prolonged exercise in irony, since whatever Folly praises is foolish and whatever she condemns is wise. Or so one might think. But in fact what Erasmus gives us is a protean work that contains numerous changes in tone, subject, and approach, so that the reader is never absolutely sure of her footing. As James McConica has aptly put it, there are "stretches [in the *Folly*] that invite the reader into a kind of intellectual vertigo."

In his dedication to More, Erasmus anticipates criticism for his sarcasm. He believes that reasonable men allow for an element of sarcasm, so long as it stays within the bounds of decency, but what really bothers him is the "sensitivity of present-day ears which can bear to hear practically nothing but honorific titles. Moreover, you can find a good many people whose religious sense is so distorted that they find the most serious blasphemies against Christ more bearable than the slightest joke on pope or prince."

Folly introduces herself to the crowd as the benevolent figure without whom the world would come to an end. Her words are credible, she argues, because "I am myself wherever I am"—being Folly, she has none of the pretensions of those who consider themselves wise. Folly goes on to prove that just about everyone can be counted as one of her followers—the old, the young, women, the gods, soldiers, artists, and scholars. After disposing of kings and courtiers, possessed as they are by obsessions with hunting, gambling, and war, Folly moves on to those who are taken in by fictitious marvels and miracle cures, those who seek imaginary pardons, magic signs and verses, and even the cult of the saints. The list of nostrums reads like a catalogue of modern therapeutic, fundamentalist, or New Age spiritual quick fixes.

Folly's take on philosophers—half-blinded by their obsession with esoteric "quiddities"—and theologians—"a remarkably supercilious and touchy lot"—could be a Dennis Miller rant about our own self-aggrandizing intellectual elites. Christ's apostles, Folly declares, would need *another* Holy Spirit, in addition to the first one, in order to teach them all the labyrinthine ideas of these scholars. Anything that leaves the clouds of abstraction and descends to earth—anything, that is, that touches on concrete human experience—is in danger of being censored by these theologians as heretical. "This proposition is scandalous," they say, "this is irreverent; this smells of heresy; this doesn't ring true."

Folly concludes her routine by celebrating the biblical passages that pay tribute to folly. Here Erasmus truly causes readers to feel a sense of vertigo. So long as Folly seemed to be praising what we "in real life" would condemn, the nature of the allegory was straightforward. But in citing the many passages in the Bible that ask believers to become like children and fools, the allegory gains a new twist. "God's foolishness is wiser than men," Folly reminds her audience. "The doctrine of the cross is folly to those who are perishing."

It is not difficult to see why the more literal-minded of his day—and ours—might find Erasmus's criticisms intemperate. To be sure, the ending appears to celebrate unlearned foolishness, and in a very real sense it does hold up the faith of the fishermen, artisans, and tax collectors who first followed Jesus. But the final irony of the *Folly* is that its celebration of simplicity is made in the most learned and sophisticated manner imaginable. Erasmus drew on the tradition of "learned ignorance," found in the work of the mystic Nicholas of Cusa and also in Dante's *Divine Comedy:* that our goal in life must be to pass from youthful ignorance through the follies of maturity and worldly involvement only to practice the imaginative and spiritual disciplines capable of restoring us to a higher form of innocence—as Dante, purged of his errors and sins, is able to glimpse, if only for a moment, the beatific vision in heaven.

The *Praise of Folly* employs irony and indirection for many reasons, but its literary artifice is ultimately used to hint at something we cannot approach directly: the mystery of God's grace. In this book Erasmus catches out the literal-minded fundamentalist on the one hand and the paganized humanist, who thinks that secular learning is sufficient, on the other. It is a sophisticated book that praises simplicity. In its love of paradox, ambiguity, and indirection, it affirms the role of art as an indispensable medium through which the transcendent can be known.

The King's Great Matter ... and Ours

THE ROYAL SOAP OPERA that is the life and reign of Henry VIII evokes endless fascination both in the realms of scholarship and the popular imagination. Erudite tomes heavy with footnotes, racy novels the size of toaster ovens, and sumptuously staged television miniseries pour forth in a steady stream. And what's not to like? For most of us, sex, power, intrigue, and those exquisite costumes are irresistible.

And yet, in all but the most superficial treatments of the period, there is a sense, whether inchoate or sharply defined, that there is more to this story than whispered betrayals in the alcoves of great halls and energetic coupling in the royal bed. "The king's great matter," as it was known in his own time—the annulment of his marriage to Catherine of Aragon, his wedding and beheading of Anne Boleyn, and the drawn-out saga of further marriages and mayhem—strike us as something familiar, recognizable, perhaps even modern. We know these characters in a way that we do not know Charlemagne or Eleanor of Aquitaine.

This came home to me as I watched the cable series *The Tudors*. The casting of a lithe young hunk as Henry had me nonplussed at first, but then I saw it. As Jonathan Rhys Meyers plays the king—lusty, charming, paranoid, and hypochondriac—I felt I could be looking at the behind-the-scenes antics of some celebrity: A-list actor, CEO, basketball star, rock legend. You can almost imagine Meyers's Henry smashing the royal furniture, if it wasn't built of solid oak.

But the resonance we feel with this saga goes deeper still. I would hazard that Henry's "great matter" takes its place alongside the fictional tales of Faust and Frankenstein as a parable of modernity, with the twist that it is grounded in historical fact. Here passion and power intersect with religion and political philosophy (the Reformation and the rise of the modern nation-state), as well as basic questions about law, freedom, and individuality.

Like Faust and Victor Frankenstein, Henry is a monster of ego who is willing to transgress ancient traditions to fill the maw of self.

What's fascinating about the many dramatic and scholarly renderings of Henry's soap opera is that while dukes and lackeys, prelates and ladies-in-waiting move across the stage, the ultimate conflict comes down to a duel between two lawyers: Thomas More and Thomas Cromwell. More was a consummate writer in both Latin and the vernacular, the author of the enigmatic masterpiece *Utopia,* and friend to Erasmus and his circle of humanist intellectuals throughout Europe. Cromwell rose from even humbler origins to become the trusted councilor of Cardinal Wolsey and, in due course, to King Henry himself. He had traveled in Europe as a young man, fought as a soldier and gone into business, and eventually came to sympathize with the Reformation.

By and large, history has been kinder to More, whose refusal to endorse Henry's marriage to Anne Boleyn cost him his head; canonized by the Catholic Church, More is regarded by many as a saint and a martyr or at the very least a hero of conscience. Cromwell, on the other hand, has been seen as a ruthless enforcer of Henry's will, a master manipulator and spymaster.

The conflict between these two men remains central to any understanding of the period, but their reputations have changed significantly in the last few decades. An increasing number of writers began pointing to More's role in the hunting down, torture, and execution of Protestant "heretics." It has also been noted that More's many polemical works against the Reformers were characterized by vitriolic, scatological language—a ferocity at odds with the playful humanist rhetoric of earlier works like *Utopia.* At the same time detailed studies have demonstrated that Cromwell was a highly competent bureaucrat who crafted much legislation that improved the governance and living conditions of England.

The shift in standing of these men has only recently emerged into the larger culture. For example, the opening essay in literary critic James Wood's highly regarded book *The Broken Estate* consisted of his own furious attack on More. It concludes that More was "cruel in punishment, evasive in argument, lusty for power, and repressive in politics."

But the publication of a new novel has brought the debate to a much wider audience. Hilary Mantel's *Wolf Hall,* which won Britain's most prestigious literary award, the Man Booker Prize, in 2009, has become a best seller, praised in reverential tones by nearly all its reviewers. The hero of

Wolf Hall is none other than Thomas Cromwell, and its villain is Thomas More.

The reviewers focus their attention on Mantel's mastery of dialogue, deftly rendered scenes, and large but sharply delineated cast of characters. At the same time, they seem to accept her premise about More and Cromwell without acknowledging that it might be controversial. Whether this is historical illiteracy or a measure of how far the changing reputation of the two men has permeated the culture is hard to say.

Wolf Hall is not frothy historical fiction, but it is more simplistic than its surface sophistication would lead one to believe. It also demonstrates that the very modernity of Henry's story makes it difficult for contemporary readers to understand what was at stake. In a very real sense, we are all Henry VIII today: autonomous individuals who fear the claims of tradition and transcendence as inherently repressive.

Wolf Hall is a radically flawed book—a sustained act of aggression that conceals its didacticism and sentimentality under a cover of toughness. The problems begin with Mantel's depiction of Cromwell, who is made into a figure of the Enlightenment *avant la lettre*. As Michael Caines wrote in the *Times Literary Supplement*, Mantel's Cromwell is "a skeptic, a modern: more our contemporary than More's, a believer in rational light. . . . He speaks of all things, from royalty downwards, with something like postmillennial skepticism, if not downright anachronistic irreverence. It seems only natural that his thoughts sometimes seem to merge with those of the narrator."

In Mantel's treatment, it is Cromwell who is the "man for all seasons"—the famous epithet given to Thomas More by Erasmus. Early on we hear that Cromwell "can draft a contract, train a falcon, draw a map, stop a street fight, furnish a house, and fix a jury." If this last ability gives you pause, it doesn't appear to trouble the narrator, who has various characters speak of Cromwell as "the cleverest man in England . . . a person of great force of will . . . the steadiest hand I know . . . a man of good cheer, liberal, open-handed, gracious." Perhaps the low point of the narrator's valorization of her alter ego comes when Cromwell asks his wife: "I've never made you cry, have I?" Her response: "Only with laughter."

On the other hand, "There is something sly in More, he enjoys embarrassing people. . . . He respects neither ignorance nor innocence. . . . He would chain you up, for a mistranslation. He would, for a difference in your Greek, kill you." Mantel's More is a cross between the Grand Inquisitor and a snotty Oxford don. "You and God have always been on familiar terms. . . .

I wonder how you dare," Cromwell intones. The low point on this side of the ledger: "They say that Thomas More is in love with his own daughter."

The sad thing is that a novel about these men could have explored the ambiguities surrounding them with much greater respect for the complexities of character and vision. They did, in fact, have much in common: both were reformers who felt that the worst excesses of the medieval church should be curbed; both believed in making education more available to the common people; both had large households that took in needy, struggling people and gave them hope. Though little is known of Cromwell's inner life, it is likely that he has been overly vilified and made into a foil for More by dramatists down the centuries.

Wolf Hall may be an overrated novel, but the problem it illustrates—the contemporary inability to understand the modern reduction of our humanity to autonomous individualism—remains. It is precisely the enigma of Thomas More that can help us here. In one of his less extreme statements, James Wood provides the starting place for reflection: "It is difficult to reconcile the author of *Utopia* with the heretic hunter of the mid-1520s."

It won't do to point out that Cromwell sent more people to the stake than More did, or that Cromwell's rationale for religious persecution had been subtly transformed from a theological to a political one (where heresy morphed into treason as the church was subsumed by the state). Nor is it sufficient to note that we should forego the anachronistic and self-congratulatory pleasure of hindsight about how sixteenth-century public servants should have avoided cruel and unusual punishments. Nor, finally, is it enough to say that the raucous style More employed in his religious polemics was part of a larger literary continuum that extends forward to writers like Milton, and that More often wrote wittily and ironically in this mode. These are worthy considerations but they don't go to the heart of the matter.

The truth is that the project of Renaissance humanism, of which *Utopia* was a dazzling example, was itself a response to the kind of reductionism that rose to the surface in the king's great matter. The late-medieval world had experienced its own crisis of faith in the sacramental nature of language and institutions. Anticipating the radical doubt of Descartes and Derrida, the medieval thinkers known as the Nominalists came to the conviction that words could no longer participate directly in the reality of things, but could only be arbitrary, isolated signs arranged in ways that we consciously will. Metaphor itself became suspect; plain, literal, and utilitarian words were better, surer things.

Humanists like More and Erasmus feared that the sort of rational-ist abstraction emerging from this crisis would itself leave people lost in solipsistic individualism and the inevitable conflicts that would arise from this privatization of meaning. They perceived that the ancient vision of the primacy of contemplative "knowing" was being replaced by activist "mak-ing," the restless activity of those who can only find meaning by imposing their will on the world.

That is why the humanists turned to literature: it offered a middle ground where knowing and making could meet—in the microcosm of art. Literature's indirection—the centrality of context, layers of meaning, irony, and linguistic play—provided a space in which the *madeness* of the artwork could reach out to and reconnect with what-is, with being itself. In the well-wrought artifact, the active joins the contemplative; human making leaves room for mystery. But a mystery that is shared. That this was a direct analogy to what took place in the mass, where human artifacts—bread and wine—were lifted up in order to be touched by the uncreated presence of God—was not lost on the humanists.

Mantel makes her Thomas Cromwell an apostle of balance and propor-tion, but even in her telling he acts only at the level of expediency. Writers like Mantel and Wood forget that the Renaissance humanists were the true champions of balance, who struggled to keep faith and reason in a healthy tension. They strove against the ideological rationalism of both desiccated Catholic scholasticism and the literalism of the radical Protestant Reform-ers. But the humanists were also the chief critics of anti-rationalism and in particular the superstitious, magical mentality of late-medieval religiosity. That was why More and Erasmus had genuine sympathy for—and were lion-ized by—many of the key figures of what would become the Reformation. Monks had plenty of reason to fear the withering wit of the humanists.

The elusive ironies that make More's *Utopia* such a difficult book to interpret exemplify the humanist literary vision. Does More endorse the utopian world he depicts or not? Are the jokes on the utopians or on us? The utopians consider gold and jewels worthless: that would seem to criticize us. But they also embrace euthanasia, which More could hardly have accepted. The answers to the questions above are both/and rather than either/or. The dance of irony keeps us on our toes.

In his book *Cosmopoiesis: The Renaissance Experiment*, Giuseppe Mazzotta discusses the creation of utopias in the Renaissance as a humanist response to the reductionism of the era. He singles out the secularized politics of Machiavelli, a writer who violently criticized utopian fictions:

> Machiavelli's desacralized, rational . . . understanding of power
> . . . also steers clear of the organization and containment of power
> made available by imaginary utopias, from Plato's *Republic* to
> More's *Utopia*. . . . This rejection of utopian visionariness is tanta-
> mount a refusal of utopias' underlying ethical imaginings. . . .
> Because power in *The Prince* is value-free, purposeless, and non-
> teleological, it comes forth as a never-ending drive that becomes
> concrete in the encounter of conflicting wills.

However terrible the abuses of churchly power may have been in the Renaissance, More read the signs of the time correctly: the Machiavellian politics of the absolute state were on the rise. In *Wolf Hall* Cromwell says openly of his relationship to Henry: "[I] open the way to his desires. That is what a courtier does." Mantel's Cromwell is ostensibly a proto-Enlightenment apostle of tolerance, as opposed to More's oppressive Catholicism, but the reality is that the privatized, value-free Machiavellianism of Henry and Cromwell cannot organize and contain power: it can only become an endless war of "conflicting wills."

For the humanists, literature and sacramental faith maintained the delicate balance between a universe of shared, purposeful meaning and the struggle to discover and agree upon that meaning. That is why they celebrated the element of play at the heart of the imagination. Mazzotta goes on to quote an important text from Plato that "identifies play with peace and rejects war, which is the radical consequence of a power-based vision. . . . Most canonical texts of the Renaissance explicitly reflect on play in its moral and metaphysical essence: from *The Courtier* to *Utopia* to *The Praise of Folly* . . . they all focus on play as the state of freedom of mind."

What Henry and Cromwell could not abide was Thomas More's freedom of mind. His silence in the face of the oaths the king wanted him to swear was rooted in a belief that this freedom could not ultimately be violated. For the lawyer Thomas More, law was like literature: it was a cultural artifact that depends on a long interpretive tradition to capture elusive truths. Law accumulates meaning—connects to its sacred source—the way a literary tradition does, through the play of interpretation within a shared universe of meaning. New laws cannot abrogate the tradition to invent out of whole cloth simply because one wants to exercise power. In *Wolf Hall* Mantel allows More to say something he is on record as having told

Cromwell: "Now you are a member of the council, I hope you will tell the king what he ought to do, not merely what he can do. If the lion knew his own strength, it would be hard to rule him."

The faithful imagination sees the world and its affairs with a double vision, as both sacred and purposeful and yet as something fallen and provisional—a child's toy—in the light of its divine origin. Thomas More's most recent biographer, Peter Ackroyd—no Catholic apologist—explains that this vision is "how he could combine ambition and penitence, success and spirituality, in equal measure. . . . More kept in fine balance these complementary vistas—of the hollowness of the world and of the delight in game. From this awareness of duality (and perhaps the duality within his own nature) springs his wit, his irony, and the persistent doubleness of his vision."

While his friend Erasmus preferred to stay out of the political arena, and thought More mistaken in getting himself entangled in that way, More was actually fulfilling the Renaissance humanist vision, which emphasized the importance of civic engagement. He was not lusty for power but he did not shrink from exercising it within the bounds of law and tradition.

The outbreak of schism, war, and political absolutism brought the humanist dream to an end. Erasmus had to go on the run and died a broken man. When More sensed that a profound revolution was in the making, he reacted with fear and anger. Because he foresaw a world in which autonomous individualism would lead to an endless war of conflicting wills, he abandoned the humanist literary mode of *Utopia* and became a polemicist. Most of what he feared came to pass.

Should More have forgone jeremiads and written more *Utopia*s in response to the king's great matter and all its ramifications for church and state? Perhaps. But it is hard to believe that Henry would have been content with that either. The wrenching irony is that More's critics, including James Wood and Hilary Mantel, demand that he should have acted with saintly detachment even while they deride his desire to become a saint. The one allegation that makes no sense, however, is the notion that More acted inconsistently. Few men in history have been as true to their visions as Thomas More.

The great matter of the present day is not whether we can return to Christendom but whether we are prepared to admit the failure of the world Henry VIII helped to usher in. The search for a social vision that moves beyond "value-free" power cannot be based directly on Thomas More's faith, but that faith—especially as tempered by humanist balance and respect for culture and imagination—can become a force for good in the recovery of shared meaning and purpose.

Becoming the Other

IN THE FIRST DAYS of May 1610, the renowned Confucian scholar Li Madou lay dying in his home in Beijing. Hundreds of the leading citizens of the Chinese capital came to pay their respects to the man whose books on ethics, mathematics, friendship, and the mysteries of life and death had been read and circulated throughout the Middle Kingdom. The visitors recalled with great affection the many enlightening conversations and debates they had enjoyed in his residence, over which their host had presided. Even as he was slipping away they remembered his dignity and generosity in welcoming them to his home—a man somehow placid and yet vibrantly alive, white-bearded, clad in his ankle-length purple silk robe and square black hat, fan in hand.

At his death, the distinguished civil servant to the Ming Dynasty Li Zhizao petitioned the emperor for the right to give Li Madou a tomb worthy of his virtuous life and intellectual achievements. The Board of Rites added a testimonial in support of the petition. An imperial edict was quickly forthcoming, granting a plot of land for a tomb to be erected near Beijing's western wall.

A few years later, the governor of the city ordered a plaque to be affixed to the tomb. Part of the inscription read: "To one who loved righteousness and wrote illustrious books, to Li Madou, Far-Westerner."

The far west from which Li Madou came was not the western extremity of the Chinese empire. It was a lot farther off. His given name was in fact Matteo Ricci, and he was born in the town of Macerata in the Italian region known as the Marche. He had come to China as a Jesuit priest, seeking to preach the gospel. He had entered from the Portuguese trading outpost at Macao, where he learned Chinese without the aid of grammars or vocabularies, which had yet to be written. His intent was to travel north to the Forbidden City in the capital of Beijing to seek permission from the emperor for missionaries to speak openly of their faith.

As it happened, the journey took nearly two decades. Welcomed in some cities and driven out of others, Ricci and his companions were at times imprisoned and beaten. Jumping out of a window to avoid a raid by a drunken youth gang bent on killing foreigners, Ricci hurt his ankle, an injury that would afflict him for the rest of his life. Often caught up in local political struggles between powerful imperial eunuchs and local bureaucrats, Ricci learned to become the soul of tact.

Encountering an ancient, civilized culture that had only experienced a couple of brief—and long-forgotten—missionary efforts, Ricci and his immediate superior chose to listen before they spoke. They looked for analogies to what they knew and who they were. And so they began by dressing as Buddhist monks, a practice the Jesuits had first followed in Japan.

But Ricci soon became disillusioned with the decadent form of Buddhism that existed in China at that time and embraced Confucianism instead, which he believed to be closer to the heart of the indigenous culture. And so he donned his long purple silk robes and studied the *Analects* of Confucius in depth.

Knowing the central place of Confucian scholarship in Chinese public culture, Ricci wrote tracts on mathematics and friendship, seeking common ground, in the belief that all human beings had an intuitive sense of the natural law.

He shared scientific instruments, clocks, harpsichords, and Euclid with his Chinese friends. While each of these things fascinated his hosts (who had their own ancient traditions of science and music), they reacted most strongly to Ricci's world map, which struck many in the insular world of China with the force of revelation.

Tactfully, he placed the Middle Kingdom at the map's center.

Ricci's approach to his mission was shaped by his Jesuit education, which was in turn shaped by a Renaissance humanist tradition grounded in rhetoric and literature. The art of rhetoric was itself a form of tact: the shaping of language that accommodated itself to the understanding of the hearer, appealed to his heart, and built bridges through analogy and metaphor.

A skeptical reading of Ricci's mission to China—and there have been a few—holds that his method of cultural accommodation was ultimately nothing more than a sophisticated mask to hide the underlying goal of proselytization.

Such skepticism is not without merit. Many in the West, including theologians, have sought to revise the way we think about our place in the world, about our need to open ourselves more consistently and generously to the existence of those who are no longer as far away as they once were, thanks to technology, war, migration, and economic need. This process has required not only a willingness to judge the imperialistic tendencies of past cultural encounters, but the drive to overcome insularity and inertia and bring about many more encounters.

Here Matteo Ricci can help us. There is no doubt that Ricci hoped for the conversion of China to Christianity, but to reduce his approach to a subtle form of imperialism is to beg important questions—and to miss just how radical his tragically short-lived vision was.

Every cross-cultural encounter involves a complex series of exchanges, a dialectic of speaking and listening. When we meet, we represent ourselves—our culture and our convictions—to the other.

The deeper question is how an authentic exchange can overcome fear and indifference, how we can become more than we are without losing a sense of what we've been.

It goes without saying that religion has had a mixed record at best in cross-cultural encounters, but that's precisely what makes Ricci's vision so valuable. It's instructive to know that Ricci had his enemies among the faithful, too, including fellow Jesuits. Not only were there accusations that he had gone native—objections to the way he dressed and wrote (not enough explicit doctrine and apologetics)—but after his death, Ricci's choice to allow converts to practice the so-called "Chinese rites" came under heavy fire. These rites were essentially civic and familial ceremonies to honor Confucius and ancestors and to ensure piety toward the traditions that had shaped the Chinese people. A century after Ricci died, the Vatican ruled that such rites were essentially religious and forbade Chinese Christians to observe them.

At that moment Ricci's Christian humanism—his confidence that the incarnation implied that all human cultures bore the imprint of God's nature and had something precious to offer the world—was defeated by the sort of triumphalism that is rightly decried today.

This conflict brings to mind *Silence,* the tragic novel by the twentieth-century Japanese writer Shusaku Endo. *Silence* bears witness to Ricci's vision by dramatizing the plight of a fictionalized Jesuit missionary named

Sebastian Rodrigues who is well-meaning but whose triumphalism is dangerous precisely because it is unconscious.

By the time of Rodrigues's arrival in Japan, the brief period of toleration for Christianity has ended. Terrible tortures have been inflicted on both Japanese converts and the priests who have served them. In addition to excruciating physical torture, the local shoguns have begun forcing Christians to trample upon crudely carved images known as *fumie* that depict Christ and the Virgin Mary. Rodrigues, like many zealous believers, feels an odd attraction to the martyr's fate, but he is haunted by the news that another missionary, Cristóvão Ferreira (an actual historical figure), has apostatized and has taken a wife.

For all his earnestness, Rodrigues is blind to the fact that the Christian faith cannot be communicated to a Japanese culture that has no reference for the strong father figure of the Western God. He observes the special devotion of the Japanese to the Virgin, but he is vaguely disturbed by it. Because of his patriarchal bias, he misses the opportunity to link the mercy of the gentle mother to God's own nature.

Rodrigues begins his mission believing that "Men are born in two categories: the strong and the weak, the saints and the commonplace, the heroes and those who respect them." This assumption seems to be borne out by the shambling, sorry figure of Kichijiro, who has previously apostatized but who begins to shadow Rodrigues on his journeys. The priest quickly associates Kichijiro with Judas. "What thou doest, do quickly," he says to himself, assuming that Kichijiro will betray him to the authorities.

Eventually Rodrigues is captured and interrogated. Just when he thinks that he will be able to receive the martyr's crown, things become complex and ambiguous. Rodrigues discovers that Japanese converts are being tortured and executed because of him. Then he is taken to meet the infamous Ferreira, whom he is prepared to loathe.

But Ferreira, for all his guilt and suffering, turns out to be a strangely compelling figure. Speaking of the Japanese who are being killed, Ferreira says to Rodrigues: "You make yourself more important than them. . . . You dread to be the dregs of the Church like me. . . . Certainly Christ would have apostatized for them."

As he faces his own agonizing decision, Rodrigues finds that Kichijiro cannot leave him alone. Like a pitiful, mangy dog, Kichijiro will not abandon the priest. Only then does Rodrigues begin to see that he and Kichijiro are alike. Only in failure and humiliation can he recognize another facet of God's nature—the hollow, sunken face of one who has known suffering and shame.

Finally, in the moment when he believes he has utterly betrayed everything he is and believes, he hears the voice of God speak to him: "There are neither the strong nor the weak. Can anyone say that the weak do not suffer more than the strong?"

The plot of Endo's novel *Silence* is an inversion of Ricci's path in that it depicts a missionary who at first lacks the capacity to embrace the humanity of the people he has come to serve. Yet the trajectory of the novel is the same as that pioneered by Ricci: the need to sacrifice what we think makes us different. Only by engaging in a sustained act of imagination can we become the other.

When Matteo Ricci became Li Madou he lost nothing essential to his inmost self. He could truly echo the words of the theologian Henri de Lubac: "When I teach my brother it is not really I who teach him, but we are both taught by God. Truth is not a good that I possess, that I manipulate and distribute as I please. It is such that in giving it I must still receive it; in discovering it I still have to search for it; in adapting it, I must continue to adapt myself to it."

WORDS AND THE WORD:
THE WRITING LIFE

The Humiliation of the Word

The following is adapted from the commencement address given to the first graduating class of the Seattle Pacific University Master of Fine Arts degree in creative writing. The ceremony was held on August 4, 2007, as part of the MFA residency that is held concurrently with Image's *Glen Workshop in Santa Fe, New Mexico.*

"In my end is my beginning."

IT IS FITTING THAT at this residency—the last for you who are graduating—we have been reading and studying T. S. Eliot's poem *Four Quartets*. For many readers, *Four Quartets* is the most powerful and resonant exploration of Christian faith in the annals of twentieth-century poetry. It is also the kind of poem that, once you fully absorb it, tends to follow you around everywhere, interpreting your life—it possesses that sort of metaphysical urgency.

This poem has been called Eliot's *Paradiso*, after the infernal visions of Prufrock and *The Waste Land* and the purgatorial fires of *Ash Wednesday*. It's not hard to see why many have used this Dantean framework to characterize Eliot's poetic career. And there are, in fact, several moments in the *Four Quartets* when we feel that we have stepped into a shaft of sunlight and caught the edge of an epiphany, a glimmer of grace in the form of children's laughter hidden in the shrubbery.

But *Four Quartets* is hardly a depiction of etherized bliss. Eliot's old, neuralgic anxieties are all still twitchily present. The "Unreal City" of *The Waste Land* reappears in the form of a Tube ride: we find ourselves, once again, in a dim, twilight world, bored and alienated, "distracted from distraction by distraction."

In Eliot's bracing, if severe, vision, even the grandest of human faculties and endowments fail to capture and hold the experience of the divine.

147

Take, for example, our capacity to use language to communicate meaning. Eliot makes a central theme of *Four Quartets* the way that "Words strain, / Crack and sometimes break" under the burdens we place on them, both because of their own inadequacy and because "shrieking voices" in the culture at large strip them of meaning through overuse and terrible simplifications.

Nonetheless, Eliot holds that literature can serve as a countervailing force to the shrill voices that are too much with us. Literature is language shaped in such a way that readers are drawn inward toward a still point, the place where mystery and beauty re-saturate words with meaning. As a ghost-poet says to Eliot late in the poem, the mission of literature is to "purify the dialect of the tribe."

Over the course of the past two years, you have experienced what Eliot calls "the intolerable wrestle / With words and meanings." How difficult and elusive that task can be, this ordering of words so that the result is a "complete consort dancing together." As you know well, every writer faces the terror of beginning, a dread rivaled only by the struggle to find an ending that achieves a sense of fullness, if not of completeness or closure.

Eliot understands these fears, but he has wrested a modicum of hope from his own long vocation as a writer: "What we call the beginning is often the end / And to make an end is to make a beginning. / The end is where we start from." By repeating the word "end" Eliot is up to his old linguistic tricks, piling various meanings on top of one another. "End" is not only a cessation, conclusion, mortality, but also a goal, fulfillment, destiny—what a thing is made for.

The Seattle Pacific University MFA is a program that dares to place the craft of writing alongside sustained reflection upon "ends." With Eliot we believe that the end of our createdness as human beings is to participate in the mystery of divine grace. Contrary to the secularist's stereotype, this is not a smug assertion but an invitation to humility, a recognition of our fragility as fleshly creatures made of humus, earth. "Humility," Eliot says, "is endless."

In the Christian tradition God insists that our salvation must come in and through the weakness of the flesh—a fact that many believers, preferring their *deus* to be *ex machina,* tend to forget. As Eliot puts it in "The Dry Salvages": "The hint half guessed, the gift half understood, is Incarnation." Or, to use Saint John's formulation: "The Word became flesh and dwelt among us."

To know one's end is not the same as having reached it. The flesh must endure passion and death before it is transformed. Therein lies the drama. Now Eliot's epigraph from Heraclitus becomes clear: "the way up and the way down are the same" because God's descent is the same as the raising of our humanity to the divine (the drama the Eastern Church calls *theosis*).

As writers, then, we can gain some confidence that our words may contain their end in their beginning. Everything we write is a "raid on the inarticulate," at once utterly insufficient and utterly necessary. And unless our words are firmly grounded in the flesh and suffer the passion of our fallen condition, they will become lifeless abstractions and join the shrieking voices that dominate our culture—and our churches.

This is the challenge you have faced. The difficulty of the task remains. But, as Eliot reminds us, there are aids that can help us persevere through our confusion and weakness: "These are only hints and guesses, / Hints followed by guesses; and the rest / Is prayer, observance, discipline, thought and action." In the course of this rigorous degree you have been given the opportunity to develop these five habits of being. May they stand you in good stead as you face each new beginning.

Stalking the Spirit

The following is adapted from the commencement address for the Seattle Pacific University Master of Fine Arts degree in creative writing delivered on August 7, 2010.

THIS PROGRAM IS BLESSED to have its intensive, ten-day residencies at two of the most beautiful places on the continent: the high desert of Santa Fe, New Mexico, and the water's edge on Whidbey Island, Washington, where we look across the Strait of Juan de Fuca at the Olympic Mountains. At the graduation ceremonies held at the conclusion of these residencies there is always a chance that nature will make a dramatic entrance. Here at our Santa Fe graduations it's monsoon season, when the thunderheads build up over the course of the day and you can see curtains of rain stretching for miles across the valley. In March on Whidbey Island the blustery early spring weather can blow in off Puget Sound with such ferocity that it can almost knock you off your feet.

We've been thinking a great deal about nature at this residency, where our Art and Faith seminar has been focused on two of the natural world's most sensitive chroniclers, Gerard Manley Hopkins and Annie Dillard.

Both writers tend to be remembered for their lyric—and occasionally ecstatic—celebrations of nature's beauty and bounty. To think of Hopkins is to recall his praise for pied beauty, "For rose-moles all in stipple upon trout that swim; / Fresh-firecoal chestnut-falls; finches' wings." Dillard's encounters with creatures of all kinds come to mind, such as her famous eye-lock with a weasel, "thin as a curve, a muscled ribbon, brown as fruitwood, soft-furred, alert."

And yet, as we've discovered in our intensive engagement with their writings, these authors can also plunge us into the horror of a shipwreck in frigid waters or a flood that carries all before it. Hopkins may help us to see the kestrel or "windhover" as a magnificent master of the air currents, but he can also write about feeling despair like a vulture that has made carrion of his soul. Dillard has a special knack for delivering up tales of insect and reptile behavior that are the stuff of waking nightmares.

That nature can encompass both heart-piercing beauty and mindless destruction has given us much to think about—raising many of the big philosophical and theological questions. But what strikes me as especially apt for this moment is that the approach to nature shared by Hopkins and Dillard provides us with analogies to the writing life itself. In the act of exploring nature's mysteries, they teach us how to write.

The process might be described as a fourfold effort involving sacrificing, seeing, stalking, and sacramentalizing.

I put those words in that order deliberately. While it might seem that seeing the world is the first step for a writer, both Hopkins and Dillard are convinced that seeing is a more complicated act than the mere opening of our eyes. They are convinced that we cannot see truly without first practicing a kind of sacrifice. The world may be charged, in Hopkins's phrase, with the grandeur of God, but that glory too often remains obscured from view.

Many things get in the way: boredom, weariness, fear, alienation—and the persistent human tendency to hold the world at a distance, to prefer the cleanliness of ideas to the capacity to be fully embodied, fully present to our experience.

In short, *we* get in the way. So what do we do about that?

Sometimes we don't have to do anything. From time to time we may be vouchsafed moments of vision that come as pure epiphany—the irruption of grace into our lives—like the tree full of lights that rocks Annie Dillard's world.

But while it is true that we cannot earn such grace, we can and must labor to place ourselves in its precincts. Hopkins understands this paradox and then reveals its cost. Describing the beauty of the night sky with its "bright boroughs" and "circle-citadels" of stars, he says: "it is all a purchase, all is a prize. / Buy then! bid then!—What?—Prayer, patience, alms, vows."

What needs to be sacrificed before we are able to see is . . . us. Or at least our selfishness and fear and abstraction. Our sense that we are detached, solitary observers. The disciplines that Hopkins says are required to purge these flaws are valuable in themselves but have their secular equivalents in the habits of the writer. Dillard agrees. She says that there is a type of seeing that is methodical and analytical but that there is a better kind "that involves letting go. When I see this way I am transfixed and emptied."

We need, she says, to regain our innocence. "What I call innocence is the spirit's unselfconscious state at any moment of pure devotion to any object. It is at once a receptiveness and total concentration."

At the very moment we lose ourselves to true seeing we suddenly realize that we are also seen. As Dillard writes in *Pilgrim at Tinker Creek*:

> I walk out; I see something, some event that would otherwise have been utterly missed and lost; or something sees me, some enormous power brushes me with its clean wing, and I resound like a beaten bell. I am an explorer, then, and I am also a stalker, or the instrument of the hunt itself. I am the arrow shaft, carved along my length by unexpected lights and gashes from the very sky, and this book is the straying trail of blood.

Dillard tells us that to get a glimpse into mystery is to become like Moses sitting in the cleft of the rock so he can get a peek at God's "back parts." The discipline needed to make that kind of seeing possible—the ability to wedge ourselves into that cleft—she calls "stalking." It demands patience—the kind of patience one needs to wait, perfectly still, in a bush for forty minutes just to catch sight of a muskrat. ("The writer should never be afraid of staring," says Flannery O'Connor.)

Now I'll grant you that there's something slightly absurd about the image of the young Annie Dillard stalking a muskrat by sitting in a bush for the better part of an hour, chain-smoking cigarettes, but she's already anticipated that. The muskrat may be a silly little thing, but perhaps another part of the sacrifice we need to make involves giving up some of our dignity and our aloofness. Perhaps we need to play the fool in order to approach even the smallest creature with something akin to sacred awe.

Dillard quotes a Hasidic master who said: "When you walk across the fields with your mind pure and holy, then from all the stones, and all growing things, and animals, the sparks of their souls come out and cling to you, and then they are purified and become a holy fire in you."

The irony here is that the writer's form of stalking generally takes the form of sitting at a computer for hours on end. Even as one's "back parts" grow numb, there is still a chance that the imagination will venture out and take its place in the cleft of memory and begin to *see*.

I sometimes say that half the value of this MFA degree is the effort we make to instill in our graduates the habit of sitting at that screen for at least a couple of hours a day.

So, when the creative writer has sacrificed self-consciousness and begun to see clearly and stalk her prey, what happens next? Here we encounter a twist in the plot.

As Hopkins and Dillard have shown us, it turns out that the creative writer's goal is *not* simply to explain the meaning of what has been glimpsed. Rather, it is to recreate—to enact—the very process of sacrificing and seeing and stalking.

The literary artifact invites the reader to enter into a collaborative search with the author. Either our writing becomes a shared journey, a participatory act, or it leaves the reader outside, looking in—reinforcing solitude and separateness.

If a piece of writing is to authentically dramatize the process of seeing, then it cannot fall into the trap of pride, the notion that the artifact can somehow be perfect and self-sufficient. Rather, it must in some sense deconstruct itself, reveal its own inadequacy. Thus Hopkins can write of the windhover's mastery of the air as an analogy for God's grandeur, only to realize that his metaphor falls short, too partial to account for the fullness of truth. He comes to a moment of recognition that the light of grace flashes out not only from rarely glimpsed majestic birds but also from the "sheer plod" of ordinary life, where a plough's blade can pass through the soil only to emerge and catch the reflection of the sun. But even that metaphor cannot bear the weight of reality and so he pictures grace as the ashy, dying ember of a fire that can suddenly crack open and reveal its red-hot heart—life emerging from death.

As the students pointed out after their group discussions on Hopkins, the movement "The Windhover" traces is essentially an act of revision—a journey of discovery—from heaven to earth, aristocratic images to those associated with the common man. The metaphors at the end invoke Christ's incarnation in the dust of this earth so that the humblest things become sacraments.

In *Holy the Firm* Dillard writes about toting wine in her backpack: "Here is a bottle of wine with a label, Christ with a cork. I bear holiness splintered into a vessel, very God of very God, the sempiternal silence personal and brooding, bright on the back of my ribs." A sacrament is meaningful not because it is esoteric but because it is ordinary; in the course of the rite the world that has been lost to us is restored. In the Eucharist the drama enacted is the movement from sacrifice to seeing. By the end we have literally been brought to our senses.

So I say to you graduates: this is the end toward which your writing must always strive, the weaving together of words so as to invite the indwelling of the Word. As you embark on your writing careers, practice self-sacrifice, see the world truly, and stalk the spirit within the flesh.

Then you will be able to confect sacraments that unite your journeys to those of your readers—and to the journey of the one who descended from air to earth, who was gashed and galled by our pettiness and vanity, only to rise again and ascend through the air, but not before he revealed through the gash in his side the burning heat of his sacred heart.

The Operation of Grace

The following is adapted from a commencement address given for the Seattle Pacific University Master of Fine Arts in creative writing on August 6, 2011.

I'D LIKE TO SHARE a few thoughts with you that I hope are appropriate for the occasion, words derived from two texts we've studied together, T. S. Eliot's *Four Quartets* and Evelyn Waugh's *Brideshead Revisited*. Both were written in the years just before and during World War II; both sought to find hope amid the encroaching catastrophe—the possibility of grace and renewal in the face of a civilization being destroyed from within as well as from without.

The war had the effect of evoking deep personal feeling in both these writers, so much so that Waugh, at least, feared he had crossed the line into sentimentality. In *Four Quartets* Eliot returns to places that had deep psychic significance for him—places associated with his childhood and family and his adopted faith. *Brideshead* evoked Waugh's escapades as a student at Oxford in the years between the wars—a time on the ambiguous cusp between the innocence of youth and a more serious, adult engagement with the world.

It might appear at first glance that the circumstances in which these books were written have little relation to the world we inhabit. But I think we should hesitate before assuming this. Our wars today may be fought in distant places, leaving our lives relatively undisturbed, but the stakes remain high. However just the cause, war is always a morally ambiguous act, tempting us to pride, the demonization of the other, and eroding our respect for human dignity.

Eliot and Waugh understood those temptations. In particular, they feared that the coarsening effect of war was reducing ancient moral bulwarks and replacing them with a utilitarian order in which the pursuit of private gain outweighed the common good. The welfare state, they came to believe, while ostensibly devoted to the common good, was ultimately little more than a mechanism for redistributing wealth; it left people locked in their alienated, private worlds.

So they sought for signs of grace in the midst of personal and social fragmentation—signs that might have the power to reawaken the modern era to its ancient sources of order. But they knew such signs were increasingly hard to see. "We had the experience but missed the meaning," writes Eliot in *Four Quartets*, a statement that applies equally to the drama experienced by the characters in *Brideshead Revisited*.

At first glance grace may appear to be the most private and isolated thing of all—the elusive moment of personal illumination when an individual is suddenly vouchsafed a sense of the meaning of things.

But for Eliot and Waugh grace could never be understood as a strictly private experience—rather, they saw it as the bridge between the private and the public realm. If grace brought healing or forgiveness or understanding, it did so in such a way as to bring the individual back into communion with the larger bodies of church and society.

The moment of grace is also the irruption of the timeless into time; it is the intersection of sacred time, kairos, with the mundane world of chronos. For the Greeks, kairos was a time in between, a moment of indeterminate time in which something special happens.

But what happens in that in-between time, that liminal space? To answer that we need to invoke another Greek term, one that grows out of both ancient philosophy and the gospels, the perception of meaning in the experience of logos. This term encompasses a rich cluster of associations, including "reason" and "word" or "speech." The prologue of the Gospel of John begins: "In the beginning was the Logos and the Logos was with God, and the Logos was God" and culminates in "The Logos was made flesh and dwelt among us."

If our lives have any order it derives from the way such encounters with the Logos enable us to perceive a pattern in our own journey through time. So, too, with the larger social order—it, likewise, gains whatever order and truth it possesses through those great epiphanies of meaning that are captured in Scripture, history, philosophy, and literature. Eliot says: "History is a pattern of timeless moments."

But as Eliot reminds us: "Human kind / cannot bear very much reality." The grace communicated through the timeless moment challenges our tendency to live autonomously as petty gods of our own kingdoms. That is why Eliot chose as one of his epigraphs for *Four Quartets* the quotation from the pre-Socratic philosopher Heraclitus: "Although *logos* is common to all, most people live as if they had a wisdom of their own."

Our tendency to lurch from living as if we have a wisdom of our own rather than being attuned to the Logos makes human life dramatic. It's the drama that Waugh renders so powerfully in *Brideshead Revisited*, as his characters set off in search of love and vocation. Charles Ryder seeks to escape the boredom of his middle-class London life through his pursuit of beauty—a beauty he also glimpses in the way the aristocratic Catholics Sebastian and Julia Flyte carry themselves. It takes great tragedy and suffering before Charles is able to see that the Flytes are also trying to escape from what they perceive as the hard expectations of their social and religious responsibilities.

Because Waugh has us see the story through the eyes of the agnostic modern man, Charles Ryder, we may also miss the moments of grace that he misses, at least if we do not perceive the author's dramatic irony. Charles is quick to notice and criticize when some members of the Flyte family treat religion moralistically, but he cannot make the connection between law and grace, between the church's understanding of human fallenness and the deeper freedom to be found when we sacrifice our desire to live autonomously.

When Sebastian becomes a hopeless alcoholic who is reduced to looking after an even more pathetic figure, a lost soul named Kurt, Charles only sees degradation, not the beginnings of love and self-sacrifice and the slow work of redemptive suffering. Later still, Sebastian becomes a hanger-on at a monastery in North Africa—a broken man, perhaps, and yet still tethered to a community, if by the thinnest of threads.

When Charles and Julia fall in love they want to live an idyllic life apart from family, faith, and even history. Julia, like her brother Sebastian, had sought emancipation from the burdens imposed by those things. But as she moves from being a callow debutante to a denizen of the *beau monde* to a divorcée who has lost a child, she begins to change. Eventually, she comes to see that her relationship with Charles is closing them off from the world. It is Julia who has to remind Charles that war will soon engulf Europe and require heroic efforts to survive. In his blindness Charles cannot see Julia's slow, reluctant, but inevitable return to the sources of order and communion she had sought to flee.

As the prophetic character Anthony Blanche tells him, Charles has reduced beauty to "charm," a superficial sentimentality that seeks to escape from the hard edges of reality. Charles has become a painter of country houses and has gone off to South America's jungles and ruins in search of the exotic, only to reduce it, once again, to charm. In a larger sense, he has confused the beauty of the great house at Brideshead with the grace and beauty that motivated its builders.

Charles isn't prepared to see that beauty and indeed grace inhere in the smallest and most mundane things. And so when the roguish Lord Marchmain returns to Brideshead to die, Charles cannot abide by the family's desire to have him anointed with the last rites. To Charles it is "mumbo-jumbo" but to the priest who comes to the house it is the sign of a human being's acceptance of his true condition as a broken creature in need of grace. The priest says to him: "Do you know what I want to do? It is something so small, no show about it. . . . I just want to ask him if he is sorry for his sin . . . then I want to give him God's pardon. It is nothing, a touch of the fingers, just some oil from this little box."

But inside that little nothing is, of course, everything. Inside that smallness is an immensity beyond our ability to imagine. It is an offer of grace.

Grace may be a gift, but the question we always have to ask is whether we are prepared to receive it. In *Four Quartets* Eliot suggests that we must practice certain disciplines if we are to perceive the meaning when we have the experience: "prayer, observance, discipline, thought and action." He goes on to suggest that art itself must practice the same disciplines if it is to capture those epiphanies of grace, both in our personal lives and in the larger realm of history.

The writer is one who uses words in such a way that they may become habitations of the *logos*, the Word. Obviously, that's a tall order. Waugh said that in his novel he wanted his words to show "the operation of divine grace on a group of diverse but closely connected characters." He admitted that such an aim was perhaps presumptuous, but for the writer of faith this is a presumption that we must risk. Anything less would involve an attempt to escape from our vocation.

What you graduates will find, I think, as you pursue this vocation, is that the difficulty of the task will inculcate a humility that will counteract presumption, especially if you practice the disciplines that Eliot recommends and which this program has attempted to form in you.

Do not allow yourselves to substitute charm for the beauty that is at once more terrible and more glorious. Approach the act of writing not as an attempt to impose meaning but as a stumbling act of exploration that may, God willing, blunder into both meaning and grace. Know that however humble your literary creations may be, they must always strive to connect their timeless moments to the timeless moments that are our inheritance as a culture and our identity as the people of God.

Who's Afraid of Geoffrey Hill?

Already, like a disciplined scholar,
I piece fragments together, past conjecture,
Establishing true sequences of pain;
For so it is proper to find value
In a bleak skill, as in the thing restored:
The long-lost words of choice and valediction.
—GEOFFREY HILL, "The Songbook of Sebastian Arrurruz, I"

OXFORD UNIVERSITY HAS A new Professor of Poetry. The post is largely ceremonial, though it does require the occupant to deliver an occasional lecture. Still, it is a significant honor, second only in the United Kingdom to that of poet laureate. First established in 1708, the professorship is an exclusive club, one that has numbered among its members Matthew Arnold, Robert Graves, W. H. Auden, and Seamus Heaney.

Geoffrey Hill won this year by a landslide. Normally that sort of margin would indicate a broad base of admiration and even affection among Oxford graduates, but in this case the appearance is deceptive. It would be closer to the truth to call this a grudging landslide—an awkward, belated acknowledgement. After all, Hill's first book, *For the Unfallen,* was published in 1958, and the brilliance of his poetry and criticism has been recognized for decades. He could easily have become Professor of Poetry at any time in the last thirty years. But it is only now, as he nears eighty, that he has been granted the distinction.

Press reports about the election were filled with descriptions of his life and work that sound more bemused than admiring. Several recounted some of the epithets often flung at Hill's oeuvre: "unbearable, bullying, intransigent, intolerant . . . mandarin and rarefied . . . warmth in these poems is like a dying sun seen through a wall of ice."

Angry and difficult: it is hard to imagine two qualities we like less in our poets today.

Hill is nothing if not a contrarian—a man born out of his time. He began publishing just as "The Movement"—whose members included Philip Larkin and Kingsley Amis—gained ascendancy in Britain, a group that stressed simplicity of diction and light, bantering irony. Into that milieu Geoffrey Hill—with his densely layered allusions and etymology-soaked language, his facility for Latin and half a dozen European languages, his obsession with violence and corruption in history and politics, and his darkly Christian sensibility—emerged like the love child of Ezra Pound and T. S. Eliot.

Half a century later, Hill never has come into fashion. Clearly he asks more of contemporary readers than they are willing to give. Despite Wikipedia and Google Translate, his foreign phrases and allusions are resented. His breathtaking erudition is reduced to the dirtiest word we can think of: elitism. His magnetic attraction to what Eliot called the "overwhelming question" causes distress.

The subjects that preoccupy Hill—the mystery of sin, our forgetfulness of the past, the enormous responsibility that rests on those who use words in the public realm, and the triumph of vanity and superficiality in contemporary culture—are considered downers these days, even in literary circles (perhaps especially in literary circles). We prefer the small, private, limpid moment to the large public stages of history—the battlefields, concentration camps, and assassination scenes to which Hill returns time and again.

And yet, for all these criticisms, few who have ever put some effort into reading Hill report that he has failed to reward them handsomely. The work he expects us to do is the best possible kind: the deep imaginative labor of making connections and understanding contexts—which, in the end, is a pleasurable form of serious play. If Hill writes about violence and tragedy, he also writes generously about those who bear witness to truth in the face of persecution or indifference, the saints and poets whose word became their bond, their baptism in blood: Dietrich Bonhoeffer, Charles Péguy, Gerard Manley Hopkins, Simone Weil.

When asked recently about the charge that his poetry is not accessible enough, Hill had this to say:

> Accessible is a perfectly good word if applied to supermarket
> aisles, art galleries, polling stations and public lavatories, but it

has no place in the discussion of poetry and poetics. Human beings are difficult. We're difficult to ourselves; we're difficult to each other and we are mysteries to ourselves; we are mysteries to each other. One encounters in any ordinary day far more real difficulty than one confronts in the most "intellectual" piece of work. Why is it believed that poetry, prose, painting, music should be less than we are? Why does music, why does poetry have to address us in simplified terms, when, if such simplifications were applied to our own inner selves, we would find it demeaning?

Hill turns the standard argument about difficult poetry being undemocratic on its head. Democracies go wrong, he says, when they are swayed by terrible simplifications. Art that keeps us alive to the moral ambiguities of life is the best protection against the slogans of ideologues and tyrants.

Hill's career as a poet began, appropriately enough, with a poem entitled "Genesis," and the powerful cadence of his voice was established in the opening lines: "Against the burly air I strode / Crying the miracles of God." As an annunciation of his lifelong preoccupations, "Genesis" is pitch-perfect:

> By blood we live, the hot, the cold,
>> To ravage and redeem the world:
>> There is no bloodless myth will hold.
> And by Christ's blood are men made free
>> Though in close shrouds their bodies lie
>> Under the rough pelt of the sea;
> Though Earth has rolled beneath her weight
> The bones that cannot bear the light.

As Hill must have known from the outset, the introduction of religiously charged language would not be a popular move. But it has remained there, stubbornly entwined not only with the poetry but the criticism as well. In an early essay—also something of a manifesto—entitled "Poetry as Menace and Atonement," Hill wrote that "the technical perfecting of a poem is an act of atonement, in the radical etymological sense—an act of at-one-ment, a setting at one, a bringing into concord, a reconciling, a uniting in harmony." Drawing on the thought of American southern poet Allen Tate and French philosopher Jacques Maritain, Hill criticized the modern sin of "'angelism,' the refusal of the creature to submit . . . to the exigencies of the created natural order." To avoid the sin of "illiberal pride . . . the speaker [of a poem] must submit to an exemplary ordeal." Only then will his language avoid the menace of narcissism and achieve "an atonement of aesthetics with rectitude of judgment." "From the depths of the self," he concludes, "we rise to a concurrence with that which is not-self."

If these concerns sound a lot like those of T. S. Eliot, that's because Hill has been locked in a protracted *agon* with that poet. While critical of Eliot on many occasions—he thinks that the *Four Quartets* represents a tragic fall into metrically weak and sentimental language—Hill shares Eliot's belief that poetry must move from self to not-self, from the present to history, from the private to the public. In his long sequence *The Triumph of Love*, Hill speaks of "*Laus / et vituperatio*: the worst / remembered, least understood, of the modes." The ancient rhetorical mode of "praise and blame" calls on the poet to engage not only in lyric celebration but also prophetic speech. At the end of this sequence, Hill concludes that poetry is "a sad and angry consolation," a paradoxical combination of grief and outrage against injustice with the bitter, healing herb of truth.

The strange, disturbing thing about the accusations of anger against Geoffrey Hill is the double standard being applied. Creative writers today are frequently lionized for their anger over such issues as global warming or civil rights. The answer, I suspect, goes back to the problem of "angelism." The form of indignation popular now stems from an externalizing of evil into institutions, governments, classes; it is expressed from an angelic height that refuses to submit to the exigencies of the created order. Hill's anger is more unsettling because it cuts to the quick of our souls; it gives no quarter because it goes to the heart of our creatureliness. Hill could say, with Aleksandr Solzhenitsyn, a writer he closely resembles: "If only there were evil people somewhere insidiously committing evil deeds, and it were necessary only to separate them from the rest of us and destroy them. But the line dividing good and evil cuts through the heart of every human being. And who is willing to destroy a piece of his own heart?"

A fascinating aspect of Hill's own life and work is that in recent years he has not only recorded his own painful submission to the limits of the human condition but developed a capacity for black comedy. After years of depression and virtual silence, Hill received treatment that has led to a late publishing bonanza. The *vituperatio* remains as sharp as ever, but now it includes himself. "Shameless old man," he calls himself in *The Triumph of Love*. "Charged with erudition, / put up by the defence to be / his own accuser."

And, if you look carefully, there is *laus*—love, even—to be found in Hill's poetry, as in the *canzoni* of praise to the Blessed Virgin in the same poem. "*Vergine bella*," he hails her, remembering her statue at the end of World War II:

> when your blast-scarred face
> appeared staring, seemingly in disbelief,
> shocked beyond recollection, unable to recognize
> the mighty and the tender salutations
> that slowly, with innumerable false starts, the ages
> had put together for your glory
> in words and the harmonies of stone.
> But you have long known and endured all things
> since you first suffered the Incarnation.

Much of the greatest poetry throughout history has been difficult. What we forget is that these works come down to us cushioned by a cloud of interpretation. That is how the economy of literature works. That responsibility lies with us. And we're late in getting started with Geoffrey Hill.

When he arrives in Oxford to deliver his first lecture as Professor of Poetry, Hill will appear stern and white-bearded, walking with a cane. But I suspect that he'll steal a brief, tender glance at the soaring steeple of the university church that stands in the High Street, dedicated to Saint Mary the Virgin, the *Vergine bella* beyond the recollection of many, but not this man.

The Poetry of Exile

HISTORY IS WRITTEN BY the victors, so the saying goes. It would be pleasant to believe that the history of literature (or the arts in general) might prove an exception to this rule, that artistic merit will always be recognized in its own time, regardless of fashion or ideology. But we know that's not true. Artists who consciously or unconsciously spurn the dominant institutions and trends of their culture always struggle to gain recognition.

There are posthumous demotions and rediscoveries, of course, which can bring about a measure of belated justice. But it's hard not to think from time to time of those who toil—and remain—in obscurity, without the hope of future resurrection.

I've been pondering this subject a great deal lately as I edit a volume of the selected poems of Dunstan Thompson.

By nearly all standards of literary achievement, Dunstan Thompson was a failure. His life and work are today known to only a few older poets and scholars, who remember the Anglo-American scene around World War II. After publishing two well-received volumes of poetry, Thompson simply dropped off the map.

In 1984, ten years after Thompson's death from liver cancer, and nearly forty years after his last published volume, there appeared *Dunstan Thompson, Poems 1950–1974*, brought out by a small British press. It went almost without notice in mainstream journals and magazines. Edited by Thompson's longtime companion, Philip Trower, this book demonstrated that, despite his vanishing from public view, Thompson continued to write poetry right up to his death.

What is so astonishing about the posthumous volume is the revelation that, despite his disappearance from the literary scene, Thompson did not lose his edge—or his passion. He continued to explore a variety of poetic forms and to pursue the only subject that he ultimately cared about: the meaning of love.

As I've labored on the editing project, I've come to think of Dunstan Thompson as a poet of exile. In the end, how much of his experience of exile was self-chosen and how much was imposed from without doesn't really matter. Thompson knew that the danger of exile was a drift into solipsism, but he decided that in his exile he would strive to live and work *sub specie aeternitatis*. Late in his life he wrote:

So this Advent waiting
Is almost done.
My poems will peer
Up through the future—
Paper flowers
Set out for everyone.
And I shall wonder
Why I worried
Lest they never
Come to bloom.

Dunstan Thompson was born in New London, Connecticut, the son of a naval officer, and grandson of a convert to Roman Catholicism. A sensitive and somewhat frail boy, Thompson was educated at Catholic schools, but by the time he reached Harvard he had rejected religious faith. At Harvard he immediately distinguished himself in literary circles, becoming the editor of the *Monthly*.

Thompson went on to edit a short-lived but lively literary magazine, *Vice Versa*, after which he joined the armed forces, ending up in London at the end of World War II. In the nine months immediately following the war Thompson underwent a tremendous amount of emotional stress. The promiscuous gay lifestyle he was leading was proving increasingly hollow. After a six-month trip to the Middle East he decided to live as an expatriate in England. Here, after he and Philip Trower had established a stable relationship, he found himself on a religious journey.

In 1952, at thirty-four, Thompson returned to the practice of the Catholic faith. Trower was also received into the church, and they were granted permission to live celibately with one another, which they did until Thompson's death.

That, in bare bones outline, is a description of Thompson's public career. What seems clear from this vantage point in time is that his conversion was twofold: religious and aesthetic. His earlier style, baroque and hothouse-romantic, gives way to a spare, classicist voice. One doesn't have to be a conspiracy theorist to see that for some these twin conversions would be interpreted as betrayals—or perhaps simply as a departure into irrelevance.

Though there is almost no self-pity in the later poems, he found the metaphor of exile apt. In "Ovid on the Dacian Coast" the exiled poet transmutes the fragmentary nature of his life into a unified and universal experience.

> The marsh birds wheel and shriek
>   Above him, as he takes
> Word after word from their bleak
>   Coast of love: his heart breaks.
>
> In place of gold, he sets
>   A banished life between
> Driftwood, and out of fish nets
>   Roofs his loss with sea green.
>
> Thus lives unexiled, though
>   Abandoned, stranded, scanned
> By the Dog Star only, for so
>   Based, his poems are his own land.

Ovid loses the world, only to gain it back through patient attendance to, and imaginative transformation of, the created order. The poet's sacrifice and suffering participate in a redemptive mission.

Thompson refuses to romanticize the poet's role; again and again he returns to the poet's self-preoccupation and temptation to stand back from harsh realities demanding love and sacrifice. In "At the Bektashi Monastery," the speaker addresses an effete poet who ignores local suffering in order to pursue refined observations about ancient ruins. The poet, sidestepping his own responsibility, wishes that the wealthy would alleviate the poverty around him. The speaker then asks:

> So is your latent love for these
> Deformed and desperate people real?
> That wizened face, it looks like yours.
> This twisted finger wears

> Your signet ring. And all the rare
> Stigmata of text-book disease
> Flower across yourself.

But the poet misses the chance at self-recognition and goes up with the tourists, leaving the beggars below "Where mystic Moslem monks who danced / Now quietly are. . . . An old calm / Dervish, with a rosary, takes your alms / And stores it in between his prayers."

That love and poverty might be related can be seen in "Three Views of Assisi," which is a triumph of simplicity. The three views are Assisi's three churches. Each poem contrasts the wealth of the churches against the poverty of Saints Francis and Clare. In the final poem the magnificent artwork of Giotto and Cimabue is set against the splendor of the ordinary down in the grotto beneath the church.

> . . . here the fluent stutter.
> And here the experts are abashed. The sound
> of praying rises like the thunder of
> A battle driven desperate underground. . . .

> Here poverty, superb, is something more
> Than riches gone. You've had your way. The poor,
> At home here, crowd your palace, then go, crowned
> In your likeness, towards that paradise
> The birds and fish still preach about, allure
> The children to. There cats are kind to mice.
> There you speak for us to il gran Signor.

The homeliness of the imagery is reminiscent of George Herbert, but has no need of metaphysical conceits to achieve its effect.

Thompson's poetry often gains greater force and tautness when there is something personal at stake. For example, "The Halfway House" is a sequence of nineteen poems based on a journey to the Nitrian Desert where the ancient monastery of the Romans, Deir al-Baramus, is located. It is a poem about conversion, using the contrast between the privation and negative way of the desert with the noise and clutter of the world. It also reminds us that the monastic vocation is itself a form of "estrangement," a self-imposed exile from the world. In section 13 the monks are described:

At night they startle snuffling beasts, who find
Them robed in sheets of stone, dissembling sleep,
Their tired eyes open on the other side
Of things. They suffer silently the deep
Estrangement they have ventured on, the friend
Who for a friend has gone alone ahead,
And prays a lifetime, speechless, in a cave
That he, repenting, may pass by the grave
Business of lying
In the desert, dying
Of want of love.

The range of Dunstan Thompson's poetic oeuvre is more varied than can be indicated here. Working on the edition of his selected poems has been a wrenching but profoundly rewarding experience. In his expatriate exile, confronting death, having given up any chance for fame or attention, Dunstan Thompson never loses his sense of humor, or his awareness of a larger world outside himself.

One of my favorites is a poem I imagine he wrote near his death. It is called "On a Crucifix," and though it was printed left-aligned in his posthumous collection, I have a strong suspicion that it is a pattern poem, like George Herbert's "Easter Wings." In this poem is distilled Dunstan Thompson's reflection on another failure—a failure, like his, that conceals a mystery, though it appears as foolishness in the eyes of the world.

See
Here at last
Is
Love

SCENES FROM A
LITERARY LIFE

The Voice of This Calling

FOUR DAYS AFTER I turned three, my sister was born. I was young enough to be confused and anxious about what was going on. My mother had grown large and then abruptly disappeared from our apartment, where I was left with a sitter. This all took place in the days when hypersensitivity about germs and infections kept small children out of hospitals. A couple of days later my father drove me to the back of the hospital in his 1957 Thunderbird convertible, the car my mother would make him relinquish in favor of a sedan that would accommodate two growing children.

Standing on a thin strip of grass between the parking lot and the hospital wall, I looked up and saw my mother leaning out of a second-story window, assuring me with a smile that she was well and that she would soon return home with my sister. Then she dropped a brightly wrapped package out of the window. In my memory it seems to tumble through the air in slow motion. Opening it, I discovered a Popeye Printing Set, complete with orange rubber stamps, an ink pad, and paper. The next thing I recall is playing with it in the bathroom of our apartment. Because it involved ink, I was only allowed to play with it there. Even now I see myself balancing the whole kit precariously on the edge of the sink, fearing that at any moment it would slip and skitter across the room.

There were stamps with crude pictures of Popeye, Olive Oyl, and the other characters from the cartoon strip along with letters and numbers. A strange joy crept over me as I arranged them in pleasing patterns on sheet after sheet of paper.

Not long after that, we moved to New York City. When she needed to shop or have a little time to herself, my mother would bring me to my father's office in the Pan Am (now Met Life) building. For hours on end I would watch him sit at a light table and create print advertisements using rubber cement and X-acto knives, arranging pictures and text on stiff boards. I wasn't allowed near the X-acto blades, but I would dip my finger in the rubber cement, twiddling the sticky stuff in my fingers until it made miniature balls that I could ricochet off the office walls.

When my father wasn't doing layout, he'd sit at his IBM Selectric typewriter, a technological wonder that reminded me of the sleek, streamlined gadgets I'd seen at the 1964 World's Fair. The Selectric was light-years beyond conventional typewriters. It was a humming, magical trapezoid, with a red matte finish and a silver globe of type in the center that would rotate at high speed to place letters and numbers on the page. My father's hands flew over the keyboard as if he were Van Cliburn at the piano.

A decade later, on a warm summer day, not long after I had been liberated from school and the rigors of a New England winter and its chilly spring, my father took me aside and made a startling request. He told me how proud he was of the writing assignments I'd done in school. Then came the bombshell. He told me that he thought it would be a terrific idea if I'd continue writing over the summer, working with him on a number of topics. He thought it would be fun.

I thought otherwise. What he had proposed went against all the laws of nature. Summers were for play, not work, I protested. He cajoled. I dug in.

As I search my memory today, I cannot recall if I ever wrote any of those essays. But it hardly matters, because when he issued that friendly challenge something deep inside me resonated with the idea. In a subconscious way, with a mixture of dread, guilt, and excitement, I knew he was right. I could write, even in the summertime.

Within a year or two I was writing poetry and op-ed pieces for the high school literary magazine and newspaper, soliciting articles and doing layout. My first publications were printed in purple, toxic ink on rotating mimeograph machines. When I went to college, I inherited the Selectric.

I've never stopped. And though Selectrics and rubber cement have been replaced by word processors and layout software, I continue to feel the same churning mixture of dread, guilt, and excitement every time I sit down to write or edit.

Vocation is a mysterious thing. It seems to come to us both from without—as a call from someone or something—and from within, as an inexplicable compulsion. It is at once a burden and a release, a responsibility and a wild, secret joy. It cannot be willed into existence and yet it demands strenuous acts of will to live out.

Simone Weil, writing about the nature of education, said that the highest virtue of learning is attention, which she likened to prayer. "Attention is an effort, the greatest of all efforts perhaps, but it is a negative effort. . . . Above all, our thought should be empty, waiting, not seeking anything, but ready to receive in its naked truth the object which is to penetrate it."

Weil's comment brought to my mind some lines from Over the Rhine's song "Latter Days," staking out a similar vision: "What a beautiful piece of heartache this has all turned out to be. / Lord knows we've learned the hard way all about healthy apathy."

The process of finding one's vocation is often fraught with fear, but that is often because we too readily equate vocation with career, with something willed, planned, chosen. It is hard to wait, to hollow out the self and thus become an echo chamber in which to hear, in T. S. Eliot's phrase, the voice of one's calling.

I recently came across a story from the desert fathers that may seem to extol the opposite of attention, and yet it somehow seems to be of a piece with Weil's insight. An old hermit who lived near Scetis suffered from forgetfulness. He went to see Abba John to seek a word of wisdom about how to be less forgetful. But by the time he made it back to his cell he had forgotten what Abba John had told him. This happened many times. Eventually the old man apologized to Abba John for taking so much of his time. The holy man replied with a question: Does a lamp suffer diminution when other lamps are lit from it? The old man said no. Abba John said that even if the whole population of the area came to him constantly, it could not diminish the flame that originates with Christ.

I'd like to think that those who follow their vocation are like that old man: always forgetting and always coming back for a word of wisdom. We may not be able to live in a perfect state of attention but we can always return and listen for wisdom. In the early years of *Image*'s history, when we only had a single pilot issue to show others as we sought the support we'd need to become a full-time publication, we often thought of quitting. We'd set a deadline, determined to give up after, say, six months. A year later we'd realize that we had forgotten the deadline. We kept right on forgetting until the journal became a reality.

Much has been made of the vocation of the artist, perhaps too much. Since the Romantic era there has been a tendency to elevate the artist's calling above other, supposedly more mundane vocations. But in a commodified culture, which values productivity over nearly everything else, it's a different story. The artist fares well in theory, but she faces an uphill battle in practice—struggling to make a living and justifying the time spent on her work.

The artist is first an observer, someone who stands apart and then reshapes experience. The products of art are, in a sense, "nothings"—gratuitous objects that serve no immediate utilitarian purpose. That they in fact serve one of the highest purposes—helping us to understand what it means to be human—often fails to impress.

Oddly, some of the most utilitarian thinking seems to take place within religious communities, where artists are frequently regarded with suspicion. I have met pious artists who have given up their vocations because, they argued, art had become an idol. But a vocation is not an idol. The self-destructive gnosticism behind such renunciations arises when people of faith come to regard desire itself as evil. But the saints and doctors of the church have always stressed that desire is the impelling force through which we return to God. "Desire alone draws God down," Weil wrote. The demands of an artistic vocation can become forms of spiritual, as well as aesthetic, disciplines.

Secularists have also done damage to a proper understanding of the artist's vocation. In attempting to make art a substitute for religion and the artist a substitute for the priest, the secular mind has forged the myth of the artist as self-creator, autonomous and sovereign.

There may have been an air of exhilaration when artists first took on the role of shaman; the glow has long since worn off. When the artist attempts to generate his own calling, he becomes Narcissus transfixed by his own image. When art is made not in answer to a call from outside the self but as its own call, the voice loses authority, becomes shrill and assertive. So much of the art that is made today is either mere virtuosity or strident propaganda.

Jacques Maritain once wrote:

> Religion alone can help the art of our epoch to keep the best of its promises, I do not say by clothing it in gaudy devotion or applying it directly to the apostolate, but by putting it in a position to respect its own nature and to take its true place. For it is only in the light of theology that art today can achieve self-knowledge and cure itself of the false systems of metaphysics which plague it. By showing us where moral truth and the genuine supernatural are situate, religion saves poetry from the absurdity of believing itself

destined to transform ethics and life, saves it from overweening arrogance.

The artist's calling is not in the wind, earthquake, and fire of human activity, but in the still, small voice that speaks through our human experience. That voice may be quiet, but it is insistent, and while it places burdens upon us, it also liberates.

Scenes from an Editorial Life

THE PUBLICATION OF THE fiftieth issue of a journal doesn't constitute an anniversary, but it does have the feel of a milestone. The impulse, especially for someone who was present at the creation, is to engage in a little fond reminiscence. Yet I find myself resisting that impulse. In fact, as the years have passed, I've found myself reflecting less on the role I've played in shaping this enterprise than on what it has done to shape me.

It goes without saying that a project as all-consuming as a quarterly journal like *Image* is the proverbial gorilla in the room. The primate is always hungry. Or, to use a metaphor that someone near and dear to me has occasionally deployed: *Image* is like a high-maintenance mistress, always demanding shopping money and prone to making indiscreet calls to the home phone number.

From time to time I find myself asking: where is the line between noble endeavor and obsessive compulsive disorder? Or monomania, for that matter?

Call me Ahab.

Several times I've asked my family to pull up stakes and move so I could take a new day job to keep *Image*—and the household—alive. At such moments the sheer weight of the journal becomes an issue: paper is *heavy*. Six years ago I drove across the continent in a twenty-four-foot rental truck packed to the gunnels with back issues. My wife Suzanne and four kids (along with the three cats and a few house plants) followed behind in the minivan, cringing at every sharp curve high in the Rockies, fearing that the force of inertia would pull the high truck over the steel railing.

Down I would go. Buried by *Image*.

As I said, good paper is heavy. And it isn't cheap. Publishing a journal of literature and the arts in an era when reading is in decline and omnipresent pop culture shortens attention spans and shrinks the human heart; investing in expensive production values in order to give art its due and demonstrate that religious faith doesn't inevitably entail shoddy work; choosing to transcend the boundaries of particular political, aesthetic, and denominational communities—these costly choices are all good things, right?

But good things contain the seeds of their own undoing.

I learned early on that the skills needed to found a journal are not necessarily the same as those needed to sustain it. And it's precisely at this pressure point where I've found myself becoming someone I did not always recognize.

Having to make the case year in and year out takes a toll. As I've sat in living rooms and corporate and foundation offices, straining to argue for the relevance and culture-transforming mission of this venture, I've found myself becoming alternately defensive and aggressive. Once, speaking to a program officer at a foundation that gave millions to churches and seminaries as well as to art museums and opera houses, I presented *Image* as the perfect synthesis of his organization's interests. "But you're not a seminary or an opera house," he said. After several variations on this exchange, my jaw started to do funny things.

In another conference room, a famous entrepreneur proudly told me that he had hired a personal trainer—of the literary sort. The trainer came to his office three days a week to take the mogul through Homer's *Odyssey*. With this promising beginning, I pitched him on *Image*. "I'm not interested in that," he replied. "The real way to change the culture is through Hollywood blockbusters."

Some people have a gift for fundraising. The late Henri Nouwen, a friend and a contributor to these pages, once gave a luminous talk on "The Spirituality of Fundraising" in which he counseled people like me to present our projects as opportunities for others to participate in the work of building the kingdom. But Henri, fundraising has always made me seize up with guilt.

When British aristocrats would get a hankering to erect some architectural monstrosity—a mini-Pantheon, say, on the hill above their stately home—it would be called a "folly." For a long time that's what I thought I was doing: building a folly. It took much longer than it should have for me to learn that I was wrong.

After years of patient counsel from friends and strangers, it finally came clear to me. It takes a measure of both confidence and humility to see that something you've helped to create has become more than a hobby horse—that it has moved far, far beyond your own part in it. A long-suffering member of our board of directors and an old friend of mine, on hearing my tale of woe one too many times, turned to me and said: "So what you're telling me, Greg, is that it's all about *you*." With a start, the truth struck home: like Ahab, I had forgotten that I was sailing on a ship with a dedicated crew—a community, really—that kept the vessel afloat and on course.

And yet, looking across the conference room table at the Homer-reading mogul extolling the virtues of Hollywood, I feel the panic rising as I wonder how to keep the good things alive, worried that at any moment I might raise my voice—or begin to weep.

Making sacrifices oneself is one thing. Asking others, including one's family, to make them is another. There has never been a day in my life when I didn't have enough to eat or a place to lay my head, but that hasn't insulated me from the financial anxieties of the middle class and middle-aged. When my home equity loan began to exceed the equity in my home and the bank began to call, I wondered what I would say at the dinner table.

I used to think that the primary emotions caused by lack were anger and fear. But through hard experience I've learned that the state of having too little is dominated, not by anger or fear, but by shame. I am grateful for this lesson, but it is not something I would wish on anyone else.

When money is tight, either at home or at *Image*, I hunker down, a survivalist holed up in a mountain cave with canned goods and a shotgun. I have invented a nickname for this persona: I call him Mr. Scrappy. Mr. Scrappy possesses some virtues, no doubt; he's a thrifty guy, a good steward of scarce resources, an efficient nonprofit arts administrator. But when he asks artists and writers—and his family—to accept something less than befits their dignity and worth, Mr. Scrappy dies a little inside.

Being an editor is not a job for those who crave popularity. To be an editor is to be a gatekeeper, faced with huge numbers of aspirants seeking publication, appreciation, love. For the editor, judgment and selection are like breathing and eating. Sadly, turning away submissions never gets any easier. In the process I've lost friendships and, what is worse, I've felt that friendships I'd like to make have been prevented by the turning down of a manuscript. In that sense, it is difficult for an editor to have the social life she might like.

The pain of rejection may lead some writers to suspect that there is something insidious at work—at best, idiosyncratic and subjective personal taste; at worst, that it's all about who you know. No set of editors, however rigorously they challenge each other, can wholly avoid an element of subjectivity in the final result. But it has been my experience that the conscientious pursuit of aesthetic discrimination *does* lead to something like objectivity, to the love of the forms through which beauty radiates. As for the second suspicion, I can honestly say that we open every envelope with a willingness to be surprised and delighted—as much when a cover letter lists no previous publications at all as when it lists *The Atlantic* or *Paris Review*. What editor doesn't want the glory of discovering a new writer?

This is where I begin to hope that fifty issues of *Image* have done something to shape me for the good. God knows there are as many rewards to this job as rigors and ambiguities. When we receive letters and emails from readers we are often astonished by their passion and eloquence in relating what *Image* means to them. Many seem to offer less a casual word of praise than something akin to a testimony.

While that undoubtedly has something to do with the quality of the journal, it also grows out of our identity as a showcase for the finest art and literature of our time, works that grapple with the moral, spiritual, and intellectual experience of the Judeo-Christian tradition. Those who respond so powerfully to *Image* do so not on purely aesthetic grounds, but out of encounters that are both aesthetic and spiritual.

When readers celebrate the combination of beauty and grace in our pages, they are describing what people have always wanted from art: not just pleasure but significance. I would be the last to suggest that the only enduring art in human history is that which directly grapples with matters of biblical revelation or transcendence. But in a time when so much of what passes for art is little more than narcissism or thinly veiled ideology, art that asks the big questions can help steer us back to a world charged with meaning.

The rewards of the job have been many, too many to list here. Over the last two decades I have witnessed more substantive and dynamic ecumenism and interfaith dialogue through my work with *Image* than I have seen anywhere else, including all the official commissions and panels. The community that has formed around *Image* remains incredibly diverse, not only in terms of denomination and geography but in its range of aesthetic styles and political convictions. Art really is able to provide a space in which people can come together and relate to one another in ways that other forms of communication often fail to provide.

Then there has been the joy of working with gifted colleagues—staff, interns, board of directors, and donors. I can say without undue self-deprecation that they receive far too little of the credit for whatever has been accomplished in the journal and our other programs. Since I can't list them all, I will single out Mary Kenagy, an enormously gifted writer and editor who has helped the journal become more fully what it always was in potential. I call her The Oracle. I think she prefers Mary.

I have to conclude with a word about my family. There wouldn't be one issue of *Image*, much less fifty, without them. Suzanne, for some unaccountable reason, decided to take on an immature recovering political junkie with a weakness for the arts and love me into becoming a wiser, better human being. Her hand is everywhere in these pages. She once received a piece of junk mail that began: "Dear Mrs. Image: Would you like to hear a little good news for a change?" She did, as it happened (the letter arrived soon after we discovered termites in the beams supporting our house), and while it may be a backhanded compliment, Suzanne truly is Mrs. Image. She and our four splendid children spend a great deal of their waking lives kicking my butt, something they find endlessly hilarious. But, as I've made clear, my butt needs that sort of treatment. They have also shown me more love and trust than I deserve, which is as close to a definition of grace as I will ever know.

The Four Cultures

AN OLD ALBERT BROOKS film has been rattling around in my head of late: *Defending Your Life*. Divorced advertising exec fiddles with the CD player in his brand new BMW and plows into a city bus, only to find himself in Judgment City, where he has to account for himself in a jury trial where the evidence consists of episodes from his life. The worst possible result isn't exactly hell; it's being sent back to earth for another attempt, rather than moving forward, to a better planet and a better life.

In the version of the film playing in my head, the judges, prosecutor, and defender all bear a striking resemblance to . . . me. Now that I am in that midway point of which Dante speaks, I find myself looking back, trying to figure out exactly how I got here. I may not be quite as lost as Dante's pilgrim in the dark wood, but I am beginning to realize one thing—just how wrong I've been in thinking I always knew what I was doing. The conscious choices I made now appear to me more like the iceberg's tip. The greater mass—my deeper self—has been below the surface, moved by currents of which I am only now becoming aware.

Like a surprise witness at that trial I've been daydreaming about, a book I read recently has gone a long way toward illuminating the direction and pattern of those currents. *Four Cultures of the West* (2004) by John W. O'Malley, SJ, is a lively, wide-ranging, historical survey of the core styles of thought and vision that have shaped our civilization. O'Malley is a church historian specializing in the early modern period; he has written about the Council of Trent and the founding of the Jesuit order of which he is a member. As it turns out, *Four Cultures* is a book he wrote in much the same spirit as I read it. In the introduction he writes: "I was curious to understand better what had happened to me in the process" of being educated as a Jesuit.

Though he is too modest a man to say it in his book, the Jesuit order was founded in the Renaissance during a remarkable period in which all four of these cultures were synthesized by Ignatius of Loyola and his

189

followers. At the outset of his story, O'Malley alludes to the early church father Tertullian's famous challenge: "What has Jerusalem to do with Athens?" In other words, what does the prophetic, religious culture of Judaism and Christianity have to do with the "worldly" cultures of ancient Greece?

The answer given by the West, as it evolved through the medieval and Renaissance eras, is: plenty. That prophetic culture was placed in dynamic tension with the academic/professional culture of the philosophers and scientists, the humanistic culture of poets, rhetoricians, and statesmen, and the artistic culture of visual and performing artists.

Father O'Malley is aware of the dangers of sweeping generalization. He concedes that there are a number of other cultures in our historic experience, business culture, for example. But he makes a compelling case for the Big Four as fundamental to our development as a civilization. In their interplay, sometimes harmonic and oftentimes antagonistic, I've come to understand a bit more about my own journey. As the privileged beneficiary of an excellent education, I was steeped in all four cultures, but I've elected to spend my life working to promote two of them because I have witnessed the other two run amok.

In his book Father O'Malley refrains from discussing any metatheory of how the cultures ought to relate to one another. Instead, he sticks to historically grounded description. At first I found this frustrating—I was hoping for some color commentary. But I came to see the wisdom of his method: he hopes that the reader will "make application to your own milieu."

My own youthful milieu embraced all of the cultures. In school I was introduced to the academic method, which is analytical and "never satisfied . . . critical of every wisdom . . . insatiably eager to ask the further question." I loved the bracing technique of bringing logic to bear on the evidence, though I found the lack of consensus on so many matters disconcerting. I came to see that academic discourse was, as O'Malley puts it, "agonistic and contentious."

In church I encountered prophetic culture, where the words of Jesus and the Old Testament prophets came from another language altogether, that of revelation—the transcendent slicing through our worldly expectations. Though its method was that of proclamation rather than reasoning, and paradox rather than syllogism, I felt instinctively that the prophetic complemented the academic, that revelation could stand up to reason, and that the foolishness of faith could keep intellectuals from excessive pride.

My introduction to cultures three and four came largely through my parents. As a former advertising executive himself, my father understood business culture, but in reality his heart lay in the tradition of what O'Malley calls "humanist culture," the province of "rhetoric, poetry, and the common good." When I was a child he turned away from business to throw himself into the realm of nonprofit causes. His gift as a writer was for the op-ed piece—language preoccupied with the first two cultures but aimed at persuasion, which is the essence of rhetoric. My father was less interested in poetry and fiction, which O'Malley notes are "more circular than linear" and glory "in ambiguity, in rich layers of meaning." But his love of words and good writing helped awaken my interest in literature.

From my mother I derived a fascination for culture four, the visual and performing arts. She took me to the Metropolitan Museum of Art and the Boston Symphony Orchestra before I could determine that these weren't cool things for a boy to like. And so they imprinted themselves on me. In discussing culture four O'Malley notes the relationship between liturgy and "ritual performance"; certainly Seiji Ozawa had the aura of a high priest as he stood, baton in hand, before the orchestra.

In my innocence, I wanted it all, the whole blessed symphony of the four cultures. And of course there was something beautiful and right in that ardent desire. (I would have loved being educated by Jesuits.) But my fall from innocence was this: I hadn't yet understood my limitations and gifts, nor had I fully grasped the state of the world around me.

O'Malley rightly stresses that the differences and clashes between the four cultures are not always about content. They are in many ways about *style,* about forms of thought and discourse. The classic example he uses is the debate between Erasmus and Luther about free will. The two men shared many ideas, including a passion for reforming the church, and yet the clash between them was not merely about ideas. Luther spoke in the language of prophetic absolutes, while Erasmus the humanist preferred caution and nuance—a number of small truths rather than Truth.

While each of the cultures has its virtues and vices, I came to fear the increasingly imperial claims of the prophetic and academic cultures—at least in the postmodern America in which I came to maturity. I have written elsewhere about the "culture wars," so I will only note here that at root, they were a conflict between extreme versions of the prophetic and academic cultures (often using the culture of the arts as an arena in which to fight their battles). One side claimed Truth through simplistic, context-less readings of the Bible, while the other deconstructed the very idea of truth (thus making their own claim to Truth).

When it came time for me to contemplate getting a PhD, something in me balked. Part of this was undoubtedly impatience, but I think I had an instinctive sense that a doctorate in literature might do something to change the shape of my mind, bending it in a direction I did not want to follow. The academic study of literature had become dominated by theory, the triumph of the academic over the literary. I wanted no part of it.

At a time when faith and reason were being abused, I was instead drawn to the common element in cultures three and four: the imagination, which shuns abstractions for the concrete. O'Malley says of the Renaissance humanists I came to admire that their imaginative genius consisted in the way they understood *context,* the layers of historical and symbolic meaning in which ideas inhere. By studying languages and the way they change, the humanists developed the disciplines of history and textual criticism.

The humanists also believed that rhetoric was the use of crafted language to speak to specific contexts. Unlike prophecy or analysis, the primary goal of rhetoric is to seek unity, common ground. Far from being ivory tower intellectuals, humanists frequently inhabit the political realm, but they do so as peacemakers, not firebrands. Finding the right word for the right occasion exemplifies this desire for unity, connection.

But consider the low regard we have today for terms like *rhetoric* and *oratory.* Their meanings have almost completely reversed, so that they now are synonymous with falsehood and verbal frippery. Such is the politicization of our times that I'm hard pressed to name anyone beyond Wendell Berry as being capable of bearing the title of orator. The two presidential candidates in the US this year have made some effort to link their use of language to more honest political visions, but it remains to be seen if either will be able to sustain this hope.

So this life I'm defending has been spent in the realm of creative writing and the arts, though never in deliberate isolation from the other cultures. In particular, I've been drawn to the ways that prophetic culture can be placed in tension with the imaginative cultures, precisely because they need each other so much. What happens when prophecy meets art, heaven meets earth—when divine imperatives meet the tangled human condition? When two cultures meet, they challenge one another, preventing them from the excesses particular to their own natures. Faith asks art to be about something more than formal virtuosity and to consider that meaning itself is already inherently metaphysical, even religious. Art asks faith to become incarnate in the human condition without compromise—or evasion—and remain compelling.

The goal should always be a communion of cultures. Father O'Malley's Jesuit tradition represents one of the noblest efforts toward achieving that. And if he is too modest to say so, I'm not.

Mugg, Hitch, and Me

WHEN I WAS GROWING up, I wanted to be Christopher Hitchens. In a manner of speaking. I didn't, in fact, learn who he was until I was in my thirties, but I can see in retrospect that Hitchens was the epitome of everything I hoped to be as a writer. My passions were political, philosophical, and literary, and it seemed to me that there could be no better life than as a prolific cultural critic who wrote bluntly and even prophetically about the follies of the age. I imagined writing long review essays of contemporary novels and biographies, laced with witty asides and skewering judgments—so many stilettos slipped in under the ribs of the literary establishment.

The irony is that if I had succeeded, I would have become a mirror image of the late Mr. Hitchens: a conservative, Christian decrier of secular, liberal pieties.

The trouble was that I had few models to emulate. Nearly all the greatest political critics of the twentieth century were on the left (Irving Howe, Lionel Trilling, et al.). There was the godfather of conservatism, William F. Buckley Jr., of course, who had a way with words and was a consummate debater, but he rarely wielded a stiletto and wasn't truly a literary critic. The other right-of-center pundits struck me, then as now, as buzzing gnats— small and annoying— unpleasant rather than incisive.

That's why I felt a nearly electrical jolt when I first encountered the British journalist Malcolm Muggeridge (1903–1990), who came to speak at my undergraduate college. Here was a man raised in a Fabian socialist household who had gone to the Soviet Union in the hope that communism would prove to be utopia-in-the-making, only to discover that Stalin was a genocidal monster. Attempting to tell this story back home, Muggeridge was ridiculed by an intelligentsia that would hear no ill about "Uncle Joe." On the domestic front, Muggeridge was fired by the BBC for the sin of writing in the early 1950s that the royal family had become a "soap opera." When he became editor of the humor magazine *Punch*, he turned a staid staple of doctor's waiting rooms into a vehicle for edgy satire. A late convert to Christianity (and even later convert to Catholicism), Muggeridge's television broadcasts with an unknown Albanian nun catapulted the woman known as Mother Teresa to world fame.

On his visit to my college campus, I served as Muggeridge's chauffeur and escort, spending many hours in his company. When I first met him I hadn't known what to expect. Rather than behaving like a guru who only wanted to pontificate, Muggeridge wanted to know all about me, asking question after question about my upbringing and interests—in that, he seemed to me true to his roots as a journalist. We talked about Russian authors we loved, especially Dostoevsky and Solzhenitsyn. A staunch critic of the Soviet Union, he nonetheless shocked me by predicting (in the late 1970s) the impending fall of the communist regime in Russia.

Later, I would spend time with Muggeridge and his wife Kitty at their cottage in Sussex, where they lived simply. They both knew the morning and evening services from the Book of Common Prayer by heart, and said them each day. While I knew that Muggeridge had been mocked for criticizing sexual liberation after a life of philandering (Saint Mugg, they called him), I could not detect any hypocrisy in this late version of himself, hard as I looked.

But I did see contradictions, some of them hilarious. After spending two decades as a fixture on television, he famously declared that broadcast news had been reduced to mindless entertainment and that he had "taken down his aerials" and junked his TV set. And yet he was addicted to listening to the news on the radio, which, because he was going deaf, he played at thunderous volume on an old stereo console the size of a refrigerator. He would offer running, coruscating commentary on these broadcasts that I often wish I had recorded.

Muggeridge was also a satirist remarkably free from personal bitterness or anger. He used to say, "It's all going to hell, isn't it?" and then fail to repress a chuckle. Over his hearth hung a framed photograph of the York cathedral, on fire after having been struck by lightning. I asked him why, and he replied that the fire had taken place a few days after a bishop who had denied the virgin birth of Christ was consecrated there. "Wrath of God, dear boy. Wrath of God."

Four years after his death, I published a biography of Muggeridge, which received a smattering of largely positive reviews. A decade later, when it was reprinted in a paperback edition, I expected no reviews. So I was surprised when a friend emailed me: "Did you know that Christopher Hitchens has written a long review of your book in the *Weekly Standard?*"

By that point I had become familiar with Christopher Hitchens from his constant flow of writing in *Vanity Fair, The Atlantic, Slate,* and elsewhere, not to mention his frequent television appearances on news and political talk shows. You can imagine that I was preparing to find a stiletto under my own ribs (which were feeling a little rubbery at that point). After all, I had cited Hitchens in the biography as one who had frequently stuck it to Muggeridge, whom he once referred to as "that old mountebank."

Sure enough, there were zingers directed at both Muggeridge and me. Hitchens writes that Muggeridge resembled a "vain old turtle" and that his voice was characterized by a "commingled bray and bleat." He cites a pledge I make at the beginning of the book that I did not want to play Boswell to Muggeridge's Johnson, uncritically recording his witty retorts and bon mots. Hitchens says that I keep to that promise throughout the book, "and I'd say that the world of the devastating riposte was not Wolfe's natural territory in any case." He also felt there was something embarrassingly gushing about my description of the Muggeridges' simple repasts, to which he adds: "and one wants to say, yes, well, that's quite enough about that."

But as I rushed on with my hurried first reading, I slammed to a halt at this sentence near the end: "Still, the cumulative effect of Wolfe's narrative in *Malcolm Muggeridge* is so serious and so genuine that the biography ultimately forces a reconsideration of its subject." Gratified as I was, I'd like to believe that part of what arrested me was Hitchens's willingness to revise his opinion about one of his favorite whipping boys. This was not the sort of concession I'd seen him make before.

What sent me back to the review was the news of Hitchens' recent untimely death from cancer. The obituaries and memorials were predictably divided, some lionizing "Hitch" for his literary brilliance and bonhomie and others deriding him as a bully and a bounder—and justifying their vitriol by saying that he was only receiving what he so gleefully dished out. Nearly all the articles had something to say about Hitchens's late-life obsession with attacking religion, which had culminated in his book *God Is Not Great.*

I went back to the review because it seemed a reasonable test case for my own estimate of his life and work, this nexus where Hitch, Mugg, and I briefly came together. To be sure, I was pleased with his conclusion, but I also knew the subject matter of his piece and could gauge the level of investment he had made in writing it.

There is no doubt that he read the book carefully: his references are detailed and accurate. The writing is as muscular as ever. But there was something else, some other quality of the review that I at first could not put into words. And then it struck me: looking at Muggeridge's life and career, he saw himself in the mirror.

After all, the parallels are abundant, from early years immersed in politics and foreign policy (including complete reversals about what they deemed to be the major geopolitical and ideological threats to the West) to later periods in which religion took over their every public statement. Both felt that George Orwell was a crucial figure—Muggeridge with a little envy and ambivalence and Hitchens with adoration. Muggeridge championed Mother Teresa; Hitchens excoriated her in his atrociously titled book *The Missionary Position*. They both began in print journalism, only to become ubiquitous on the telly.

In the review Hitchens takes note of my exploration of Muggeridge's ambivalence toward his upbringing—embarrassment at his lower-middle-class father's homemade political philosophy, desire for a more cosmopolitan, fashionable life, and yet persistent engagement with the larger social and moral issues of the day. "One of the several merits of [Wolfe's] biography . . . is that its author . . . understands this duality of motive. . . . No serious person is without contradictions. The test lies in the willingness or ability to recognize and confront them."

Christopher Hitchens may not have been willing to recognize or confront the duality of his own motives, but in this book review seems awfully close to doing so. Because in the end he must have realized that he, like Muggeridge, had to a great extent squandered his strengths as a writer and political observer to become a hectoring preacher and a stern moralist in the trivial media circus that dominates the airwaves. Of Muggeridge he says: "He was drawn compulsively to that which he found loathsome."

And yet, in and among the various potshots, Hitchens can write this of Muggeridge's youthful hunger for faith: "He was still a long way from Roman Catholicism, but his quest for the 'inclusive'—for a reconciliation between the sacred and the profane, as well as between the simple and the difficult—already involved catholicity." That longing for an inclusive vision is what endears Muggeridge to me, even as the process of writing the biography revealed to me his many faults and flaws. Muggeridge's own autobiography is entitled *Chronicles of Wasted Time,* a recognition and confrontation of his shortcomings if there ever was one. If Hitchens ever achieved a similar recognition, I've haven't seen it.

As for me, I found that by the time I had finished the biography, I had learned a thing or two about my own duality of motive. I had lost the desire to lay about me in the public square, in part because I sensed the enormous vanity it would require. Perhaps that's the thing about duality: once you sense how deeply divided the human heart is, you lose the sort of swagger and singularity needed to be the scourge of the age. I have looked in vain for the wisdom of atheism on the subject of duality, but my faith tells me all about it. And drives me toward an inclusive vision that reconciles divided peoples and riven hearts.

Breath

The wind bloweth where it listeth, and thou hearest the sound thereof, but canst not tell whence it cometh, and whither it goeth: so is every one that is born of the Spirit.
—JOHN 3:8

THE SUMMER OF 1968, though it mourned the recent assassination of Martin Luther King Jr. and shuddered at the murder of Robert F. Kennedy, was a pastoral idyll for a nine-year-old boy who had just moved from an apartment in Manhattan to the lush north shore of Long Island. My mother, concerned about crime and eager for her two children to be able to run and play in wider, greener places than urban parks, had convinced my father to rent a two-hundred-year-old farmhouse on seven acres in Kings Point.

That farmhouse has long since been torn down, and three gleaming modern homes now sit on that plot of land, but in 1968 I could still run out the back door and through a gate in an ancient, spreading grape arbor into fields rampant with blackberry canes. I quickly graduated from climbing the apple tree in our front yard to a huge pine whose close-packed branches enabled me to ascend as high as the roof of the house.

And yet there was trouble in paradise. The heavy, humid air of Long Island, thick with pollen, and the long-haired German shepherd my mother had brought home one day made it difficult for me to breathe. In my memory this was the year when I first learned that I had something with the oddly spelled name "asthma." I recall trying to pronounce the word phonetically, laboring slowly through the consonants as I labored to take in air. The condition also made me susceptible to bronchitis, which would lay me up in bed for days on end.

In that era the only way to treat asthma at home was fairly brutal. My father showed me a nebulizer made of complex glass tubing; when you squeezed the rubber ball at the bottom it would send air through the thing.

He then took a vial of epinephrine—pure adrenaline—and poured a few drops into a part of the nebulizer, explaining that I needed to compress the rubber ball and inhale at the same time, taking the spray into my lungs.

Taking anything into my lungs other than air seemed a violation of some kind, and I might have gagged a few times, but eventually I managed the feat. What came next was even more shocking. The drug dilated the passages in my lungs by forcing my heart to beat at an accelerated rate, causing my chest to thump with a raw, burning sensation.

Nonetheless, the relief it gave was very bliss.

Asthma proved a blessing of sorts because it became a bond with my father, who suffered a more extreme form of the condition. So when I was struggling he would be the one, rather than my mother, to look after me. He was usually so deeply absorbed in his work that the attention he gave me at such times was itself a balm. As I lay in bed, propped up by a mountain of pillows because it made breathing easier, he would read to me from the Bible, especially his favorite passage in the Gospel of John, chapters 14 to 17—what the scholars call the "farewell discourses" of Jesus.

"Let not your heart be troubled: ye believe in God, believe also in me," he would begin. "I will not leave you comfortless . . . the Comforter, which is the Holy Ghost, whom the Father will send in my name, he shall teach you all things, and bring all things to your remembrance, whatsoever I have said unto you."

Sometimes, if my father continued on for a few chapters, I would hear: "Again Jesus said, 'Peace be with you! As the Father has sent me, I am sending you.' And when he had said this, he breathed on them, and saith unto them, Receive ye the Holy Ghost."

The image of Jesus breathing on the disciples, which I could never quite picture but which I never doubted, haunted me then as it does now. Perhaps for obvious reasons I've always loved the sensation of wind blowing on my face, that extra bit of oxygen coming my way. One of my fondest childhood memories is of leaning out of a speeding taxicab window and basking in the rushing air after my parents had taken me to dinner in New York City one balmy summer evening.

As is often the case with physical disabilities, asthma led me into habits of concealment and occasional spasms of shame. When my gym teacher asked me why running the mile took me over seven minutes I mumbled something inaudible and skulked off to a corner of the athletic field. There were times when in my adolescent oblivion I simply forgot to take my inhaler with me—or an asthma attack overwhelmed my ability to complete a football practice.

There have only been a couple of times when asthma made me really afraid, both taking place in water: one when I capsized a canoe in a freezing river and the other when I swam out in the Gulf of Mexico as a storm rolled in and was nearly dragged down in the undertow. As often as I tell myself that I don't fear death, I find it difficult not to imagine it as a kind of suffocation.

These days my medicine comes in the form of a small plastic disc from which I inhale tiny crystals that often prevent an attack for a whole day— without any burning or thumping in my chest. But while I am grateful for another advance in modern medicine, there is seldom a moment when I am not at least subliminally conscious of breathing—a small buzz of awareness humming within me as my lungs labor on.

Zen Buddhism and other traditions stress the importance of conscious breathing techniques as a form of "mindfulness," but in one sense I'm already there.

In his novel *Breath*, the Australian writer Tim Winton tells the story of an adolescent boy growing up in a sleepy mill town near the ocean and the way surfing the huge waves off the coast becomes a form of risk-taking that dances along the edge between epiphany and death by drowning. The book is narrated in the first person retrospectively, after the protagonist in middle age has become an EMT and has taken up the didgeridoo, the playing of which requires circular breathing:

> Honking away on my old didj, I think about the one I first saw nestled against the boards in that big hippy house. I hardly knew what it was. Now the wind comes through me in circles, like a memory, one breath, without pause, hot and long. It's funny, but you never really think much about breathing. Until it's all you ever think about. I consider the startled look on the faces of my girls in the moments after each of them was born and suctioned and forced to draw air in for the first time. I've done the job myself on more than one occasion. Always the same puzzled look, the rude shock of respiration, as though the child's drawn in a gutful of fire. Yet within a moment or two the whole procedure is normalized, automatic. In a whole lifetime you might rarely give it another thought. Until you have your first asthma attack or come upon some stranger trying to drag air into himself with such effort that the stuff could be as thick and heavy as honey.

That consciousness is what always made me susceptible to those passages in the Bible, such as the Gospel of John, that speak of God's presence as breath, spirit, wind. In the Hebrew Bible the term *ruach ha-kodesh* means something like "holy spirit," though Robert Alter prefers to translate Genesis 1:2 with the more metaphorical "God's breath hovering over the waters," noting that the same word elsewhere refers to an eagle "fluttering over its young." My colleague Jack Levison, in a forthcoming book, writes: "Translations miss out on the drama of the Hebrew. Ezekiel repeats the word, *ruach*, in order to emphasize that the one and only *ruach* of God inspires the resurrection of Israel—a resurrection that is at once a personal creation like Adam's (*ruach* = breath), a cosmic rush of vitality (*ruach* = winds), and a promise of national faithfulness (*ruach* = Spirit)."

So many passages in both Hebrew and Christian Scriptures hinge on this metaphor—from the breath that God breathes into the clay that is Adam to that moment when Christ breathes on his disciples, re-creating their humanity. That which is life-giving is also invisible, both within us and outside of us, blowing where it listeth.

The theologian and spiritual writer Hans Urs von Balthasar has written about the Holy Spirit in a manner that speaks to my deepest intuitions about body, soul, and cosmos: "The Spirit is breath . . . and therefore he wishes to breathe only through us, not to present himself to us as an object; he does not wish to be seen but to be the seeing eye of grace in us, and he is little concerned about whether we pray to him, provided that we pray with him, 'Abba, Father,' provided that we consent to his unutterable groaning in the depths of our soul. He is the light that cannot be seen except upon the object that is lit up."

Groanings I have known, but with my asthma and my faltering prayer life it would be more accurate to speak, in a comic vein, of the wheezings of the spirit.

There was a time during my high-school years in Massachusetts when being on the basketball team (even as a lowly third-stringer) helped me get into the best aerobic shape of my life. A friend and I would occasionally go running at night in the colder months, when the New England air was piercing and clean.

On one winter evening the normal limitations of our bodies seemed to fall away and we began to run farther and faster than we ever had before. My strides felt like the looping arcs traced by an antelope in full flight. The stars overhead, like pinpricks in a curtain blocking a blinding light, bore down on us. Suddenly, many miles into our run, my sarcastic, lapsed-Catholic friend—the friend who used to boast to me about getting to second or third base with girls—turned to me (the naturally religious child) and said: "Let's say the Lord's Prayer."

So there, along a back road in Duxbury, Massachusetts, we two boys loped along under starlight, inspired—taking huge lungfuls of air that seemed to fill every corner of our bodies, pumping adrenaline that was entirely natural, returning glory to Father, Son, and Holy Ghost in plumes of air that came from a world without end.

Acknowledgments

THE THANKS I HAVE to offer vary little from book to book, in large part because I have been blessed by living in the midst of a stable, loving, creative community. My deepest thanks, as always, go out to my wife, Suzanne, and to my children—Magdalen, Helena, Charles, and Benedict. I am deeply indebted to *Image*'s managing editor, Mary Kenagy Mitchell, for all that she has done for the journal and for me. Along with my wife Mary has edited all of these essays—most at the last minute (my bad) and under the pressure of deadlines—and so I have chosen to dedicate this book to her. Sara Arrigoni helped me prepare the manuscript with her usual grace and efficiency. My other colleagues, current and recent—Julie Mullins, Beth Bevis, Dyana Herron, Anna Johnson, Taylor Olsen, Tyler McCabe, Aubrey Allison, and Stuart Scadron-Wattles, as well as a host of bright young interns—have inspired and supported me. Indeed, the community that has sprung up around *Image* has generated a vibrant and expansive conversation that nurtures me in countless ways. My friends Jon Stock and Jim Tedrick at Wipf & Stock Publishers have been both patient and encouraging. Jim and Bev Ohlman once again provided hospitality on Orcas Island while I completed this book. Thanks, as ever, to my companions in Communion and Liberation for their friendship and love. All of these good souls have manifested the operation of grace in my life.